A CHRONICLE OF CRISIS

2011 - 2016

ZYGMUNT BAUMAN

SOCIAL EUROPE EDITION

Dedicated to the memory of Zygmunt Bauman

CONTENTS

ABOUT THE AUTHOR

Zygmunt Bauman was Professor of Sociology at Leeds University and one of Europe's leading sociologists and public intellectuals.

ON ZYGMUNT BAUMAN

By Neal Lawson

Zygmunt Bauman, who died on the 9th January 2017 aged 91, was often spoken of as the most influential sociologist of his era. Born in Poland, he had lived in the UK since 1971, settling in Leeds where he was professor of sociology until 1991, and subsequently emeritus. It was in his 'retirement' that a crescendo of writing and talking poured out of him. Better known outside the UK, a vast array of thinkers and activists have been guided by his brilliant mind.

Bauman's big idea is that of liquid modernity. He described a society somewhere between the solid modern structures and cultures of the early to mid 20th century and the relativism of post-modernity. The era of secure jobs and institutions through which we navigated our lives with pretty well ease and certainty was being lost, giving way, some saw, to the supposed melting into air of post-modernity, where everything was entirely relative. In describing this half-way house as liquid, Bauman echoes Antonio

Gramsci's idea of the morbid symptoms that appear in the interregnum when the old is not yet dead and the new is not yet born. One of the many metaphors deployed by Zygmunt for these liquid modern times was one of skating on thin ice – a life in which only speed stops us from falling through into the icy waters below.

This breathless, insecure and exhausting notion of liquid modernity is then encapsulated in the second big shift identified by Zygmunt: from a society that essentially reproduces itself through production to a society based around consumption. Once upon a time, we knew ourselves, and each other, by what we did, now it is by what we buy. Here the metaphor is of a society epitomised not by the savings book, with its slow and steady build-up of resources to buy cherished or necessary items, but by the instant gratification offered by the credit card. In the consumer world we compete with each other to be the finest purchasers of things we didn't know we needed, with money we don't have, to impress people we don't know. Sadly for us there is no end point to this endeavour. It is a race without end. So why do we run it?

The Bauman book that had the most influence on me is *Work, Consumerism and the New Poor*. In it he describes this shift from production to consumption and through it the effect on 'the poor'. In a producer society the poor undoubtedly suffered. But they suffered together, in communities of solidarity, and they were kept just fit, healthy and educated enough to act as a reserve army – for war or any upturn in the economy. It may be temporary or cyclical but society needed them. To be poor in a consumer society is to be totally unnecessary. If we are defined by what we buy, then what is the point of you if you cannot afford to shop? The poor in such a society are merely teased (or worse) as they window-shop their way through a life of perpetual humiliation in which even the bonds of class have evaporated. It is why 'the poor' cherish the brands they can get their hands on by fair means or foul – to be 'normal' for a moment.

But the poor today do have a role, as Zygmunt sharply identifies, and it is to police us. They are 'othered', humiliated and despised to act as a warning to the rest of us, to never fall off the consumer treadmill into the abyss of the only thing worse than a life on that treadmill - the life of not being on it. More than anything we fear joining the ranks of the undeserving poor.

Why has this happened and why has so little been done about it? Zygmunt knew. In *In Search of Politics* he exposes the separation of politics from power, and power from politics, as financial flows and corporate investment escaped the nation state and its legal jurisdiction and went global. All this and more drew a line under the solid and predictable culture of the 20th century and sent us hurtling into the fragility and fluidity of a 21st century culture where everything feels temporary and until further notice.

In all this work Zygmunt understood the crisis of social democracy, whose success was rooted in the old solid jobs, fixed identities and bounded nation states. What is the role for a party called 'Labour' if what defines us is consumption? How could we be fully human when the bonds of solidarity were stretched to breaking point in a consumer race in which enough is never enough?

Zygmunt's books and essays are not always easy to read. The language can be opaque, but the shafts of light and insight are intense. The analysis is bleak, but uplifting if you believe it to be accurate. For how can we begin to wrestle with the precarious and insecure world we live in unless we understand the scale of the problems we face?

His work is followed by many. He could pack any university lecture hall in Europe and did. His many books and articles avidly read, especially amongst the young. But he never influenced the established political classes. Not yet anyway.

He was loath to set out a blueprint for the more humane society he desired. The one idea he would go back to again and again was universal basic income. Today the idea of such a citizen's income is featured regularly in articles in the *Financial Times* and elsewhere, was on the agenda of the 2017 World Economic Forum at Davos and is being trialled in Canada, Finland and the Netherlands. The Bauman Institute at Leeds will stoke the fires of his ideas, as will myriad thinkers and activists across the globe who have been captivated by his haunting insights. He was an avid writer on the Social Europe website and believed passionately in the European cause.

All of these themes – liquid modernity, the end of the producer society, poverty/inequality, the Other, the decline of the nation state and the need for transnational political union and Europe – as well as others such as migration, the false sense of community on the Internet, right-wing populism and economic nationalism find their place here in this collection of twenty-four contributions he wrote for *Social Europe* from 2011 until his death. Many of them are wonderfully prescient about what was/is coming. They all pay testimony to his genius.

Zygmunt kept thinking and writing, right up until the end (his last piece here written just eight days after Donald Trump's shocking victory). He remained what the Germans call a *Vordenker,* constantly in touch with contemporary cultural references and forward in his thinking as he crafted his arguments.

He was a frail and slight man but had an enormous

sense of intellectual power, generosity and fun. In his ramshackle, books- and papers-filled house on the edge of Leeds, as he served you vodka at noon and brought through an endless supply of Polish snacks, you knew you were in the presence of greatness. The abiding image that fills my mind when I think of this small man and his huge intellectual power, is that of Jedi master Yoda. In all the bleakness of his analysis, Zygmunt provided hope where there was only despair. He told us quite simply: 'the good society is the one that knows it is not good enough'.

Neal Lawson is chair of Compass, the cross-party campaign for the Good Society, and was author in 2009 of 'All Consuming' (Penguin), a book inspired by and dedicated to the work of Zygmunt Bauman. One of his proudest moments was to give a talk to mark the opening of the Bauman Institute in Leeds.

PART I

DISRUPTED SOCIETY

1

ON THE OUTCAST GENERATION

17 January 2011

Every generation has its measure of outcasts. There are people in each generation assigned to outcast status because a 'generation change' must mean some significant change in life conditions and life demands likely to force realities to depart from expectations implanted by the conditions-quo-ante. These changes devalue the skills they trained and promoted, and therefore render at least some among the new arrivals, those not flexible or prompt enough to adapt to the emergent standards, ill-prepared to cope with novel challenges and unarmed to resist their pressures. It does not, however, happen often that the plight of being outcast may stretch to embrace *a generation as a whole*. This may, however, be happening now.

Several generational changes have been noted during the post-war history of Europe. There was a 'boomer gener-ation' first, followed by two generations called respectively X and Y; most recently (though not as recently as the shock of the collapse of Reaganite/Thatcherite economics), the impending arrival of the 'Z' generation was announced. Each of these generational changes arises from more or less traumatic events; in each case, a break in continuity and the necessity of sometimes painful readjustments, caused by a clash between inherited/learned expectations and unanticipated realities, were signalled. And yet, when looking back from the second decade of the 21st century, we can hardly fail to notice that when confronted with the profound changes brought about by the latest economic collapse, each one of those previous passages between generations may well seem to be an epitome of inter-generational continuity.

Indeed, after several decades of rising expectations, the present-day newcomers to adult life confront expectations *falling* – and much too steeply and abruptly for any hope of a gentle and safe descent. There was bright, dazzling light at the end of every one of the few tunnels which their predecessors might have been forced to pass through in the course of their lives; instead, there is now a long, dark tunnel stretching behind every one of the few blinking, flickering and fast fading lights trying in vain to pierce through the gloom.

Intergenerational inequity

This is the first post-war generation facing the prospect of downward mobility. Their elders were trained to expect, matter-of-factly, that children will aim higher and reach further than they themselves managed (or had been allowed by the now bygone state of affairs) to dare and achieve: they expected the inter-generational 'reproduction of success' to go on beating their own records as easily as they themselves used to overtake the achievement of their parents. Generations of parents were used to expecting that their children will have a yet wider range of choices (one more attractive than another), be yet better educated, climb yet higher in the hierarchy of learning and professional excellence, be richer and feel even more secure. The parents' point of arrival will be the children's starting point – and a point with yet more roads stretching ahead, all leading upwards.

The youngsters of the generation now entering or preparing to enter the so-called labour market have been groomed and honed to believe that their life task is to outshoot and leave behind the parental success stories, and that such a task (barring a blow of cruel fate or their own, eminently curable inadequacy) is fully within their capacity. However far their parents have reached, they will reach further. Or so they, at any rate, have been taught and indoctrinated to believe. Nothing has prepared them for the arrival of the hard, uninviting and inhospitable new world of downgrading, devaluation of earned merits, doors showed and locked, volatility of jobs and stubbornness of joblessness, transience of prospects and durability of defeats; of a new world of stillborn projects and frustrated hopes and of chances ever more conspicuous by their absence.

These last decades were times of unbound expansion of all and any forms of higher education and of an unstoppable rise in the size of student cohorts. A university degree promised plum jobs, prosperity and glory: a volume of rewards steadily rising to match the steadily expanding ranks of degree holders. With the coordination between demand and offer ostensibly preordained, assured and well-nigh automatic, the seductive power of the promise was all but impossible to resist. Now, however, the throngs of the seduced are turning wholesale, and almost overnight, into the crowds of the frustrated. For the first time in living memory, the *whole class of graduates* faces a high probability, almost the certainty, of ad-hoc, temporary, insecure and part-time jobs, unpaid 'trainee' pseudo-jobs deceitfully re-branded 'practices' – all considerably below their acquired skills and eons below the level of their expectations; or of a stretch of unemployment lasting longer than it'll take for the next class of graduates to add their names to the already uncannily long job-centres waiting lists.

A capitalist society like ours, geared in the first place to the defence and preservation of extant privileges and only in distant (and much less respected or attended to) second to the lifting of the rest out of their deprivation, is high on goals while low on means. The graduate class has no one to turn to for assistance and remedy. People at the helm, on the right or the left side of the political spectrum alike, are up in arms in the protection of their currently muscular constituencies – against the newcomers still slow in flexing their laughably immature muscles, and in all probability deferring any earnest attempt to flex them until after the next general election. Just as we all, collectively, regardless of the peculiarities of generations, tend to be all-too-eager to defend our comforts against the livelihood demands of yet unborn generations.

While noting that 'anger, even hate' can be observed in the class of 2010 graduates, political scientist Louis Chavel, in his article published in the 4th January 2011 issue of *Le Monde* under the title '*Les jeunes sont mal partis*', asks how much time will it take to combine the rancour of the French contingent of baby-boomers infuriated by the threats to their pension nests, with that of the graduate class 2010 who have been denied the exercise of their right to earn pensions. But combine into what, we may (and should) ask? Into a new war of generations? Into a new leap in the pugnacity of extremist fringes surrounding an increasingly despondent and dejected middle? Or into a supra-generational consent that this world of ours, prominent as it is for using duplicity as its survival weapon and for burying hopes alive, is no longer sustainable and in (already criminally delayed) need of refurbishment?

2

ON SUSTAINABILITY: THIS TIME OF SOCIAL DEMOCRACY

28 January 2011

Social democrats: do they know where they are aiming? Do they have a notion of 'good society' worth fighting for? I doubt it. I believe they don't. Not in the part of the world we inhabit, at any rate. Former Chancellor Gerhard Schröder is on record squinting at both Tony Blair's and Gordon Brown's estates and saying, quite a few years ago, that there is no capitalist or socialist economy, only good or bad. For a long time now, at least thirty to forty years, the policy of social democratic parties has been articulated, one year of neoliberalism rule after another, by the principle 'whatever you (the centre-right) do, we (the centre-left) can do better'.

Sometimes, although not very often, a particularly outrageous and arrogant initiative taken by the rulers provokes a pang of old socialist conscience. It's at such times that, without making a big issue out of it, for 'those who need it most' or a 'softening of the blow' for those 'whom it hits most', more compassion and a longer lifeline are demanded – but of course not before it has been tested for prospective electoral popularity – and even more frequently by borrowing the phrases and vocabulary of 'the other side'.

This state of affairs has its reason: social democracy has lost its own separate constituency – its social fortresses and ramparts, the enclosures inhabited by people at the receiving end of political and economic actions, waiting and yearning to be recast or lift themselves from the collection of victims into an integrated collective subject of interests, political agenda and political agency all of its own. Such a constituency has been all but pulverised into an aggregate of self-concerned and self-centred individuals, competing for jobs and promotions, with little if any awareness of the commonality of fate and even less inclination to close ranks and demand solidary action.

'Solidarity' was a phenomenon endemic to the now bygone society of producers; it is but a nostalgia-bred fancy in the society of consumers. Members of this brave new society are notorious for swarming the same shops on the same date and hour, ruled now by the 'invisible hand of the market' with the same efficiency as when they were herded onto factory floors and in front of assembly lines by bosses and their hired supervisors.

Lost time and tribe

Recast as consumers first and producers a distant (and not necessary) second, the former 'social democratic constituency' dissolved in the rest of the aggregate of solitary consumers, knowing of no other 'common interest' as that of the taxpayers'. No wonder that the extant heirs of social democratic movements have their eyes focused on the 'middle ground' (not so long ago referred to as the 'middle classes') – and rally to the defence of the 'taxpayers' no longer, ostensibly, divided by their interests and so being the sole 'public' from which a solidary electoral support seems plausibly obtained. Both parts of the current political spectrum hunt and graze on the same ground, trying to sell their 'policy product' to the same clients. No room here for a 'utopia of one's own'! Not enough, at any rate, in a space separating one general election from the next.

'The left' - so José Saramago noted on 9th June 2009 in his diary – 'does not appear to have noticed that it has become very much like the right'. But it has indeed become 'very much like the right'.

A movement that in the past succeeded in representing one of the greatest hopes for humanity, capable of spurring us to action by the simple resort of an appeal to what is best in human nature, I saw, over the passage of time, undergoing a change in its social composition, ... daily moving further away from its early promises, becoming more and more like its old adversaries and enemies, as if this were the only possible means of achieving acceptance, and so ending up becoming a faint replica of what it once was, employing concepts to justify certain actions, which it formerly used to argue against. It has sold out to the right, and once it realises this, it can ask itself what has created the entrenched distance between it and its natural supporters – the poor, the needy, but also the dreamers – in relation to what still remains of its principles. *For it is no longer possible to vote for the left if the left has ceased to exist.*

It is the right, and the right only, that with the left's consent assumed the uncontested dictatorship over the political agenda of the day. It is the right that decides what is in and what is out, what can be spoken and what ought/must become/remain unspeakable. It is the right, with the connivance of the left, that draws the line separating the possible from the impossible – and thereby has made self-fulfilling Margaret Thatcher's sentence of there-being-no-alternative to itself.

The message to the poor and needy cannot be clearer: there is no alternative to the society that makes room for poverty and for needs stripped of the prospects of satisfaction, but no room for dreams and dreamers.

3

ON BUILDING FORTRESSES UNDER SIEGE

7 March 2011

Pat Bertroche, running for American Congress on behalf of Republicans in the state of Iowa, proposed on his blog that illegal immigrants ought to have microprocessors grafted into their bodies: after all, he explained, I may graft a micro-processor in my dog's body, if I wish to be able to find it. Why not do the same to the illegals? Indeed, why?

In recent European reports from the scenes of massive clashes between pro-democratic protesters and the forces defending dictatorial regimes throughout the Arab world, two types of information took pride of place. One was the plight of the citizens of the reporting countries: their lives are in danger; they should be as soon as possible moved away at a safe distance from the spots of inflammation, from the southern to the northern coast of the Mediterranean; to make it happen is the government's most urgent task, any delay is criminal. Another was the danger of the northern coast of the Mediterranean being flooded by the refugees running for life away from the battlefields of civil wars raging on the southern coast; to stop it is the government's most urgent task, any delay is criminal.

One could hear similarly deep sighs of relief in the two simultaneously transmitted and reported news items from blood-soaked Libya: of the boat packed with British evacuees mooring at La Valetta, and the crowds of Libyans running for shelter – but towards the Egyptian and Tunisian borders. The first reaction of the Italian government to the news of the change of regime in Tunisia was sending additional navy units to guard accesses to the Italian island of Lampedusa to stop Tunisian asylum seekers. And now Francois Fillon, the French prime minister, has announced that France will send to liberated Benghazi two planes with medical help. Nice gesture – you would say – testimony to our solidarity with the gallant fighters for democracy, and our willingness to join them in the battle. You would say that – unless you read Fillon's own explanation: this is one of the measures to stop the wave of immigrants threatening to flood the Mediterranean countries; the best way to stop it is to make sure that the situation in Libya will soon stabilise.

Schengen's dark side

It would be easy, but wrong, to explain that as extraordinary events or emergency measures. For almost two decades the policy of the Schengen countries on the northern side of the Mediterranean was to 'subsidiarise' the detection and confinement of the would-be immigrants inside their native countries or those native countries' immediate neighbours on the southern coast; in virtually every case, the 'bilateral agreements' were signed or entered into unofficially with tyrannical and corrupt regimes, profiting – alongside the gangs of unscrupulous smugglers – from the misery of the impoverished and persecuted exiles, thousands of whom never managed to cross the sea in gangster-supplied, over-crowded, un-seaworthy dinghies.

And yet one cannot but note that the regular strictness of the European immigration and asylum laws grows ever stricter while the toughness of the stance taken towards successful and prospective asylum-seekers grows also – all this has no connection with the unrest spreading from Tunisia to Bahrain. On the sudden hardening of Nicolas Sarkozy's posture towards the aliens recently turned Frenchmen or Frenchwomen, Eric Fassin, distinguished anthropologist and sociologist, commented in *Le Monde* that its purpose is to make the rest of Frenchmen and French-women 'forget the defeat of the President's policies on all fronts – from (falling) purchasing power to (rising) insecuri-ty', and most particularly to use the politics of national iden-tity as a cover-up for replacing social protection with the market-operated free-for-all.

Nothing new here, to be sure. The aliens inside (and particularly the domesticated ones among them), and aliens at the gate (and particularly those who have good reasons to be let through), have been by now firmly fixed in the role of usual suspects. Whenever another public inquiry of a successive misdeed or misdemeanour, failure or flop in the governing circles, is initiated – such aliens are the first to be brought to the police station, filmed avidly and shown on TV with the frequency of the memorable videos of the hijacked aircraft hitting the twin World Trade towers. In the footsteps of the picking on the immigrants-generated internal security problems as the most urgent tasks of the French government, came the decision to put the biggest of the big-wigs at the helm of foreign affairs, interior affairs and defence departments. The meaning of the reshuffle was promptly spelled out by the President in a way leaving nothing to imagination: 'My duty as the President of the Republic is to explain the future stakes, but above all to protect the present ones of the French' and this is why I've decided to 'reorganise the ministries dealing with our diplomacy and security'. And so such persons have been appointed as are 'prepared to confront future events whose course no one can predict'.

Sarkozy's islamophilia

In the good old days of 2003/2004 when prices of stocks and real estate climbed sky-high by the day, GNP figures were going up and those of unemployment stood still, when the wallets in the middle classes' pockets and in the pockets of those hoping to join them went on swelling with credit cards, Nicolas Sarkozy's voice warmed up whenever he spoke of '*l'islam de France*', of France's diversity, multiculturalism, even affirmative policy or positive discrimination, and their role in assuring peace and friendship in *les banlieues*. He would not bear with the populist habit of picking up Islam as a peculiarly suspect phenomenon demanding particularly watchful attention. In his *La République, les religions, l'espérance* (published in 2004) Sarkozy pointed out that Islam is one of the great religions, that France of 2004 is no longer an exclusively Catholic country, that it had become a multicultural nation, that instead of assimilation one should rather speak and worry about integration, which is a totally different kettle of fish: unlike the now abandoned postulate of 'assimilation', the policy of integration does not require of the newcomers the renunciation of what they are. Even in 2008, when dark clouds were already covering the notoriously blue French skies, the President, as Eric Fassin reminds us, emphatically condemned the principle of 'consanguinity', demanding to replace it with that of 'equality of chances', pointing out that 'the best medicine against communitarianism (*communautarisme*; in French discourse is the concept of the population split into autonomous and partly self-enclosed and self-governing communities) is the Republic delivering on its promise'.

Well, it is an altogether different ball game now, to borrow an American idiom. It all started in the early 2010s with the hue-and-cry after the Roma settled in Grenoble; Roma are, aren't they, the first among the first as the usual suspects go. But the Roma incidents have proved by now but modest *hors-d'oeuvres*; more to the point, mere appetisers. For once, the presumption of symmetry between '*ceux qui arrivent*' (the arrivals) and '*ceux qui accueillent*' (their hosts), underlying until recently the pronouncements transmitted from government buildings, has all but disappeared. No longer is respect required of both sides in equal measure. Respect is now due solely to France, and paying respect is the duty of the *accueillis* (the 'received') – *bien* or *mal* (well or badly), does not really matter. French community (whatever that may mean), so the announcements announce, does not want to change its way of living, its lifestyle. But the unwritten condition of those 'received' remaining 'received' is that they do change their mode of life – whether they want it or not. And, in line with the habit already noted to be the trademark of modern hypocrisy by the great Frenchman Albert Camus (a Frenchman whose personal contribution to the glory of France is next to no one), the evil is once again done in the name of good, discrimination is promoted in the name of equality, and oppression in the name of freedom. For instance: 'We don't want to compromise on little girls' right to attend schools'.

Identity and security

This is a thorny issue, no doubt... This is why the slogans 'no tolerance to the enemies of tolerance' or 'no freedom to the enemies of freedom' sound so convincing. They do – as they take for an axiom what had yet to be proved, as they pre-empt the question whether the side whose condemnation and suppression that slogan is meant to legitimise are indeed guilty of the transgressions of which they stand accused, and as they omit the question of the prosecuting rights as well as glossing over merging, illegally, the prosecutor's and the judge's roles. But does indeed the prohibition of wearing headscarves in school help to entrench the 'little girls' right to attend schools'?! André Grjebine of *Sciences Po-Centre d'études et de recherches internationales*, in the same issue of *Le Monde* ('*S'ouvrir à l'autre: oui. A son idéologie: non*') noted that 'the alterity, perceived generally as the source of spiritual openness, can be as well a carrier of fundamentalism, obscurantism and closure'; would not he, however, agree that his order of reasoning, with all its appearances of impartiality and *sine ira et studio* intention, is already a judgment in its own right, only disguised? He did not mention, after all, that 'the spiritual closure, perceived by some as the carrier of identity and security, is all the same the source of fundamentalism and obscurantism' – a connection at least as real as the one he preferred to put to the fore. Nor did he say that much as the presence of spiritual openness in some may push some others to closure, it is the *absence* of spiritual openness that offers the invariable and infallible mark of all and any fundamentalism. More often than not openness encourages, promotes, and nourishes, openness – whereas closure encourages, promotes and feeds closeness.

Amin Maalouf, the Lebanese author writing in French and settled in France, considers the reaction of 'ethnic minorities', that is to say immigrants, to the conflicting cultural pressures which they are subjected to in the country to which they have come. Maalouf's conclusion is that the more immigrants feel that the traditions of their original culture are respected in their adopted country, and the less they are disliked, hated, rejected, frightened, discriminated against and kept at an arm's length on account of their different identity – the more appealing cultural options of the new country appear to them, and the less tightly do they hold on to their separateness. Maalouf's observations are, he supposes, of key importance to the future of inter-cultural dialogue. It confirms our previous suspicions and conjectures: that there exists a strict correlation between the degree of perceived lack of threat from one side, and the 'disarming' of the issue of cultural differences from the other – this as a result of overcoming impulses towards cultural separation, and the concomitant readiness to participate in the search for common humanity.

All too often, it is the sense of being unwelcome and guilty before committing a crime; threat and uncertainty (on both sides of the supposed frontline – among the immigrants and among the indigenous population alike) are the principal and most potent stimulants of mutual suspicion followed by separation and breakdown of communication: of the theory of multiculturalism degenerating into the reality of 'multi-communitarianism'.

4

ON JUSTICE, AND HOW TO KNOW IT IS THERE

16 March 2011

In his essay *Justice in the Global World*, as before in his study *The Idea of Justice*, Amartya Sen does not beat about the bush when analysing the lessons to be drawn from the 2008 global economic slump.

Whereas some very opulent persons saw their fortunes somewhat diminished, it was the poorest people, people 'at the bottom of the pyramid', local or global, that have been affected most badly: 'Families who were already worst placed to face any further adversity have often suffered from still greater deprivation, in the form of lasting joblessness, loss of housing and shelter, loss of medical care, and other deprivations that have plagued the lives of hundreds of millions people'. The conclusion, Amartya Sen asserts, is all too obvious: if you want to correctly evaluate the severity of the current global crisis, examine 'what is happening to the lives of human beings, especially the less privileged people

– their well-being and their freedom to lead decent human lives'.

Chronically deprived categories of people tend to learn to accept their lot and just because of its 'ordinariness, indisputability, normality' suffer it meekly ('underprivileged people without hope of liberation often try to do just that to cope with the inescapability of the deprivation involved'). It is in times of crisis that the routine, daily, perpetual and habitual distribution of privileges and deprivations is abruptly recast as 'extraordinary', a fatal accident, emergency – and so brutally drawn to the surface and brought into dazzling light for everyone to see. We may add that with catastrophes affecting, as a rule, different categories of people unequally, it is the degree of vulnerability to all sorts of natural, economic or social earthquakes, the high probability of being hit much more severely than other residents of the country or other members of humanity, that is revealed as the defining feature of social injustice.

Categorical non-imperative

But wouldn't we rather begin with defining the standard of justice, so that we would be better armed to spot and isolate the cases of injustice whenever and wherever they appear (or rather hide)? Easier said than done. Amartya Sen would not advise one to take this line. Asking what the perfect justice would look like is 'a question in the answer to which there could be substantial differences even among very reasonable people'. Obviously, we may add, as reasonable people seasoned in the art of argumentation and rhetoric are to be found in every one of the camps determined, in a bizarre reversal of Kant's categorical imperative, to flex the proposed universal standards so they may fit their anything but universal interests; in other words, to summon the idea of justice to the defence of a particular injustice that rebounds as their privilege.

There is little hope, then, that a debate about universal standards of justice will ever bear fruits palatable to everyone involved and so acquire genuine universality. But there is another reason to be doubtful as to advisability of such debate. As Barrington Moore Jr. pointed out a long time ago, historical evidence shows beyond reasonable doubt that whereas they are quick in spotting injustice in the acts changing the extant state of affairs or the heretofore binding rules of the game, people tend to be abominably slow if not downright inept in decrying as 'unjust' even much more adverse conditions that they had come already, because of their persistence, to accept as 'normal', intractable, immune to protests and resistant to change.

Just like in the apparently opposite case of 'pleasure', of which Sigmund Freud observed that it tends to be felt solely at the moment when a displeasure is removed but is hardly ever brought by continuous presence of 'objectively' even the most pleasurable (that is, displeasure-free) state of affairs. In the language of semiotics, we may say that the 'injustice' as well as displeasure are contrary to appearance the primary, 'unmarked' terms of the oppositions in which 'justice' as well as 'pleasure' are the 'marked' members, that is such concepts derive all their meaning from their opposition to the 'unmarked' ones. Whatever we may know or imagine of the nature of 'justice', we derive from the experience of injustice – just as from the experience of displeasure, and only from that experience, we may learn or rather imagine what 'pleasure' may look like. In a nutshell: whenever we imagine or postulate 'justice', we tend to start from cases of injustice currently most salient, painful and offending.

Just society

Starting as we are from widely varied experiences and sharply, often irreconcilably differing interests, we are unlikely ever to arrive to an uncontentious model of the 'just society'. Not able to resolve the quandary, we can only agree to a 'settlement solution' – reduced to the hard core evident to all while staunchly unprejudiced and desisting the temptation to preempt the future twists and turns of the continuing (indeed encouraged to continue) polyvocal debate. I'd suggest, as a 'settlement' of that kind, the following formula: 'Just society' is a society permanently sensitive and vigilant to all cases of injustice and undertaking to take action to rectify them without waiting for the search of the universal model of justice to be completed. In somewhat different and perhaps simpler terms, a society up in arms to promote the well-being of the underdog; the 'well-being' including in this case the capacity of making real the formal human right to decent life – recasting 'freedom *de jure*' into 'freedom *de facto*'.

Implied in this choice of settlement formula is a preference given to Richard Rorty's 'politics of campaign' over its competitor, the 'politics of movement'. The latter, the 'politics of movement', starts from assuming an ideal model of, if not the 'perfectly' ('perfectly' meaning an *a priori* impossibility and undesirability of any further improvement) then at any rate a 'comprehensively' or 'fully' just society, and consequently measuring/evaluating any proposed move by its impact on shortening the distance separating reality from the ideal, and not by diminishing or increasing the sum total of human suffering caused by present injustices. The first, the 'politics of campaign', follows an opposite strategy: it starts from locating an indubitable case of suffering, proceeds to diagnose the injustice that caused it, and then undertakes to correct it – without wasting time on the (admittedly hopeless) attempt to solve (the admittedly irresolvable) issue of the possible impact of this undertaking on bringing the 'perfect justice' closer or delaying its arrival.

5

ON INTERNET, SLANDER, AND
IRRESPONSIBILITY

14 March 2011

Reviewing in the *NYT* of 3rd January a collection of studies edited by Marta Nussbaum and Saul Levmore and published under the title *The Offensive Internet,* Stanley Fish follows the line taken by most of its contributors – who mapped the topic of the reviewed study, the issue of anonymous slander licensed by internet vs. the demands of its legal prohibition or limitation, within the freedom of speech frame.

Can one stand up against the glorious legacy of the First Amendment, known to assume that freedom of speech cannot be overprotected, and demand that voicing of certain opinions should be made illegal and punishable? The Supreme Court Justice John Paul Stevens dismissed in 1995 the potentially morbid consequences of anonymity of information, arguing within the same frame and in the same spirit: he insisted that 'the inherent worth of ... speech in terms of its capacity for informing the public does not depend upon the identity of its source, whether corporation, association, union, or individual'.

Jürgen Habermas, by the way, would certainly, and rightly, disagree with that somewhat stretched and skewed interpretation of the First Amendment: his own theory of (ideal, undistorted) communication rested on the (empirically confirmed) supposition that precisely the opposite is true for the offering of and perceiving/absorbing/evaluating a message: most commonly, routinely, indeed matter-of-factly, we tend to judge the value of the information by the quality of its source. This is why, as Habermas complained, communication tends to be, as a rule, 'distorted': who said it matters more than what has been said. The value of an information is enhanced or debased not so much by its content, as by the authority of its author or messenger.

What inevitably follows is that in case the information arrives without the name of its source attached people are likely to feel lost and unable to take a stance; under condition of distorted communication, naming the source is an enabling act, allowing to decide whether to trust or ignore the message – and all or almost all communication in our type of society belongs to that 'distorted' category (to free itself from distortion, communication would require genuine equality of participants – equality not just around the debating table, but in the 'real', offline or off-the-debating-chamber life). Such a condition would require nothing less than exploding and levelling up the hierarchy of speakers' authority; telling people that information needs to be judged by its own, not its author's merits or vices. Stanley Fish obliquely, and in an idiom different from Habermas's, admits that fact:

Suppose I receive an anonymous note asserting that I have

been betrayed by a friend. I will not know what to make of it – is it a cruel joke, a slander, a warning, a test? But if I manage to identify the note's author – it's a friend or an enemy or a known gossip – I will be able to reason about its meaning because I will know what kind of person composed it and what motives that person might have had.

All these suggestions and reservations are, however, in this case side issues only; what really matters is whether the issue of internet-propagated and internet-enabled anonymity of opinion needs to be at all put, judged and resolved within the framework of *freedom of speech*, or whether its true social importance, one that needs to be put and kept in the focus of public concern, is its relation to the problem of a *person's responsibility* for her/his actions and for their consequences.

Net responsibility of nobody

The genuine adversary/alternative to the internet-style anonymity is not the principle of freedom of speech, but the principle of responsibility: internet-style anonymity is first and foremost, and most importantly socially, an officially endorsed licence for irresponsibility and a public lesson in practicing it – online and offline alike – an enormously large and venomous anti-social fly let free to scurry through enormously huge barrels of ointment advertised, and allegedly dedicated, to promote the cause of sociality and socialising.

The more potentially deadly the weapons, the more difficult it should be to obtain a permission to possess and carry them (though no blank-cheque permission, whether liberally or sparingly granted, should embrace its uses).

Internet (alongside the bygone 'Wild West' and the mythical jungle) is, however, a stark exemption to that rule widely assumed to be indispensable for the civilised life. Slander, invective, calumny, slur, smear, casting aspersion and defaming belong to the deadliest of weapons: deadly to persons, but also to the social fabric. Their possession and use, particularly indiscriminate use, is a crime in the offline life (commonly called 'real life', though it is far from clear which one, the online or the offline life, would win the competition for the title of reality); it's not a crime, though, in the online world. And it is all but a matter of guessing which of the two worlds, online or offline, is due to assimilate to the other and adjust its rules to the other's standards; which one will eventually surrender to the pressure, and which one will be pressed to surrender.

For the time being, though, the online world has a considerable advantage over its competitor: in the online world, unlike in the offline one, everybody can be a 007. In the online world, everyone can boast a licence to kill. Better still: everyone can kill without an effort as trifle as that of applying for a licence. It's impossible to deny the seductive power of such an advantage. And remember that each kind of seduction pre-selects its seduced.

A 'floating responsibility' (that is, responsibility detached from its carriers and agents relieved of their responsibility) means, as Hannah Arendt warned a long time ago, 'responsibility of nobody'.

6

ON THE SHAKY PROSPECTS OF MERITOCRACY

21 March 2011

The most prestigious academic institutions issuing the most prestigious academic diplomas – institutions most generous in granting social privileges or recompensing social depriva- tions – are year by year, one step at a time yet consistently and relentlessly, drifting out of the 'social' market and distancing themselves ever further from the throngs of youngsters whose hopes for glittering prizes they kindled and inflamed. As William D. Cohan informs in the *NYT* of 16th March, the annual price of tuition and fees at Harvard rose annually by 5 per cent for the last 20 years. This year, it has reached $52.000. 'Generally speaking, in order to pay just Harvard's tuition, someone would have to earn more than $100,000 in annual pre-tax compensation. And there are all the other family expenses – among them, the gaso- line, the mortgage, food and medical expenses... Very quickly the numbers get astronomical'.

And yet... of the 30,000 applicants to Harvard last year,

only 7.2 per cent were admitted. Demand for places was – still is – high. There are still thousands of parental couples for whom the tuition fees, however exorbitant, are not an obstacle, and going to Harvard or another elite academic establishment is for their children just a routine matter: the exercise of inherited right and fulfilment of family duty – the last finishing touch before settling in one's legitimate place inside the country's elite of wealth. Though there are still thousands or more parental couples ready for whatever financial sacrifice is required to help their children in joining that elite, and making thereby their grandchildren's place in the elite a legitimate expectation.

For the latter, whom the universities, turning away from their imputed/claimed role of social mobility promoters, wounded most painfully in their parental ambitions and their trust in the American Dream, Cohan has words of consolation: he suggests that perhaps 'the best and brightest among us will always find a way to achieve their inevitable level of excellence, *with or without the benefit of a traditional education*' (italics added). To make that promise sound plausible and believable, he adds an impressive and fast growing list of new billionaires, from Steve Jobs, founder of Apple, down to the Twitter inventor Jack Dorsey and the founder of Tumblr David Karp – all without exception education dropouts (with Karp beating the record by spending not a single day on campus since dropping out of a high school in his first year). Well, with secure industrial employment no longer on offer, the unemployed may always play lotto, can't they?

Shattered dreams

A high-class diploma from a high-class university was for many years the best investment which loving parents could make into their children's and children of their children's future. Or at least it was believed to be such. That belief, like so many other beliefs combining into the American (and not just American) Dream in the gates wide open to all hard working people determined to push them open and persisting in keeping them open, is now being shattered. The labour market for holders of high education credentials is currently shrinking – perhaps faster yet than the market for those lacking university certificates to enhance their market value. Nowadays, it is not just people failing to make the right kind of effort and the right kind of sacrifice who find the gates, expectedly, being shut in their face; those who did everything they believed to be necessary for success are finding themselves, though in their case unexpectedly, in much the same predicament, having been turned away from the gate empty-handed. This, to be sure, is an entirely new ball game, as the Americans use to say.

Social-promotion-through-education served for many years as a fig leaf for naked/indecent inequality of human conditions and prospects: as long as academic achievements correlated with handsome social rewards, people who failed to climb up the social ladder had only themselves to blame – and only themselves on whom to unload bitterness and wrath. After all (so the educational promise suggested), better places were reserved for people who worked better, and good fortune came to people who forced it to be good by diligent learning and a lot of sweat on the brow; if a bad fortune was your lot, your learning and your work were obviously not as good as they should have been. That apology for persistent and growing inequality is, however, sounding nowadays all but hollow. Yet more hollow than it otherwise could have sounded, were it not for the loud proclamations of the advent to the 'knowledge society', a kind of society in which knowledge becomes the prime source of national and personal wealth and in which, accordingly, the possessors and users of knowledge are entitled to that wealth's lion's share.

The shock of the new and rapidly rising phenomenon of graduate unemployment, or graduate employment much below graduate (proclaimed to be legitimate) expectations, hits painfully not just the minority of zealous climbers – but also the much wider category of people who suffered meekly their unappetising lot, numbed by the shame of missing the chances waiting in abundance for those less work-shy than themselves. It is difficult to say which of the two category-specific blows can and will cause more social damage, but together, appearing simultaneously, they make quite an explosive mixture... You can almost see quite a few people at the helm shuddering while reading Cohan's sombre warning/premonition: 'One lesson to be learned from the recent uprising in the Middle East, especially in Egypt, is that a long-suffering group of highly educated but underemployed people can be the catalyst for long overdue societal change'.

Gaining knowledge

You think this is but one more American idiosyncrasy? You well may think so, as one of the most conspicuous features of the American Dream is the belief that in the US things can occur that elsewhere, in more mundane lands, are all but unimaginable. To preempt such misconception, let's jump therefore a few thousand miles to the east of Eden: to Poland, a country that in the last two decades experienced an exorbitant rise in the number of higher education establishments, their students and graduates, but also in the costs of education – alongside a similarly spectacular rise in income polarisation and overall social inequality.

What follows is a handful of samples from an extraordinary amount of similar cases, as reported on 19th March by the Polish leading daily, *Gazeta Wyborcza*:

Two years ago Agnieszka graduated with a degree in finance and banking. Her countless job applications remained unanswered. After more than a year of invariably vain efforts and deepening despair, a friend fixed her up with a receptionist job. Among her not especially exciting duties is to collect day in, day out, the CVs of other graduates bound to remain, like hers, unanswered. Tomek, graduate of another prestigious college, did not have Agnieszka's luck and had to settle for the job of an estate guardsman for the equivalent of £280 monthly. His colleague from the same graduation ceremony is determined to take any job, if in a few more months nothing remotely related to his acquired and certified skills comes his way. All in all, more and more graduates are putting their university diplomas among the family memorabilia and settle for the not-much-skill-demanding jobs of couriers, shop assistants, taxi drivers, waiters (the latter, promising to fatten thin wages with customers' tips, gaining most in popularity...)

From Hudson to Vistula, much similar sights and sounds; the same deafening clatter of gates being shut and locked, the same off-putting picture of rapidly rising heaps of frustrated hopes. In our societies of allegedly knowledge-powered and information-driven economies and of education-driven economic success, knowledge seems to be failing to guarantee success and education failing to deliver the success-guaranteeing knowledge.

The vision of the toxins of inequality neutralised, made liveable-with and rendered harmless by the education-driven upward mobility, and yet more disastrously, the vision of education able to keep upward social mobility in operation, begin to simultaneously evaporate. Their dissipation spells trouble to education as we know it. But it also spells trouble to the excuse favoured and commonly used in our society in the efforts to justify its injustices.

7

ON THE NEW LOOKS OF INEQUALITY

4 April 2011

Frank Rich, a leading *NYT* op-ed columnist, observed recently: 'economic equality seemed within reach in 1956, at least for the vast middle class. The sense that the American promise of social and economic mobility was attainable to anyone who sought it...' That was, he reminds his readers not counting on their memories, the nation's mood 55 years ago.

As to the American middle class of today, Rich needs only ask a purely rhetorical question: 'How many middle-class Americans now believe that the sky is the limit if they work hard enough? How many trust capitalism to give them a fair shake?' – meaning how many Americans managed to preserve and retain the old trust, so much alive still a mere half-century ago: the trust in 'social equality of mobility', or 'equality on the move', 'equality coming nearer and nearer', 'equality within reach'... A rhetorical question it is indeed, since in this case Rich can rely on his readers to answer, unhesitatingly: not many. This is, roughly, what has happened to the middle-class dream 'that everyone can enter Frontierland if they try hard enough, and that no one will be denied a dream because a private party has rented out Tomorrowland'.

One day earlier another *NYT* op-ed columnist, Charles M. Blow, noted the latest statistical evidence: 'According to the National Centre for Children in Poverty, 42 percent of American children live in low-income homes and about a fifth live in poverty. It gets worse. The number of children living in poverty has risen 33 percent since 2000. For perspective, the child population of the country overall increased by only about 3 percent over that time. And, according to a 2007 UNICEF report on child poverty, the U.S. ranked last among 24 wealthy countries. The reaction to this issue in some quarters is still tangled in class and race: 'no more welfare to black and brown people who've made poor choices and haven't got the gumption to work their way out of them'.

There is no need to tell the parents of 42 percent of American children, struggling as they are day in, day out, trying to make ends meet, that the prospects of equality are nowhere nearer their children, while parents of the 20 percent of children living in poverty would hardly understand what the 'chances', of the vanishing of which the latest figures inform, were supposed to mean. Both categories of parents, however, would have little if any difficulty in decoding the message flowing loud and clear from the lips of those who set the laws of the land and translate them into the language of rights and duties of that land's citizens. The message is simplicity itself: this is no longer a land of opportunity; this is a land for people with gumption.

Renting out Tomorrowland

The socially manageable 'equality of mobility' foundered having hit the hard rock of inequality of individual gumption. Their, the parents', 'gumption' is the only life-boat on offer to those who wish to navigate their children out of poverty. A small boat this is; you'll be lucky to procure a boat capacious enough to accommodate the whole family. More likely, only a few of the family members, the most daring and tight-fisted among them and so with the largest supply of gumption, will manage to squeeze into the dinghy and keep their place for as long as it takes to reach the coast. And the journey is no longer (if it ever was) a voyage to equality. It is a chase to leave others behind. The room at the top is pre-booked and only the chosen are admitted. As Frank Rich aptly puts it, 'a private party has rented out Tomorrowland'. Land of opportunity promised more equality. Land of people with gumption has only more inequality to offer.

The Spirit Level, the eye-opening Richard Wilkinson's and Kate Pickett's study that demonstrated and explained why 'greater equality makes societies stronger', is at long last beginning to worm its way into American public opinion (thanks to Nicholas D. Kristoff's comment in the New Year issue of the *NYT*). The delay all the more thought-provoking as, for the US, the country firmly perched at the very top of the global premier league of inequality (according to the latest statistics, the wealthiest one per cent of Americans masters more wealth than the bottom ninety per cent), and one that supplied the researchers with the most extreme instances of inequality's collateral damages, Wilkinson-Pickett's message should have sounded most urgent and closest to the red-alarm level.

Even at this late stage Kristoff prefers to introduce the authors of the study to the American readers as 'distinguished British epidemiologists' (rather than connecting them to social studies, redolent as they are in the opinion of American opinion leaders of the condemnable and contemptible leftist-liberal bias and for that reason dismissed before being heard, let alone listened to). Guided probably by the same prudent caution, Kristoff quotes from the reviewed study mostly the data concerning macaques and the relations between low- and high-status macaques and other, unnamed 'monkeys'. And having quoted for support John Steinbeck's sentence on the 'sad soul' that is able to 'kill you quicker, far quicker, than a germ', he placates the possible alarm of readers spying out a tax-hike menace, and pre-empts their violent protests, by setting the bad news in the less wallet-threatening order: the toll of inequality, he points out, is 'not just economic but also a melancholy of the soul'. He admits though, even if in a somewhat round-about and innocuous way, that 'economic' it is as well, when pointing out that the choice is between less inequality and more prisons and police – both alternatives known all too well to be costly in rates-of-tax terms.

Biology, stupid!

Inequality is bad not as such, not because of its own injustice, inhumanity, immorality and life-destroying potential, but for making souls bad and melancholic. And for its morbid connection with biology, now finally scientifically confirmed: 'humans become stressed when they find themselves at the bottom of a hierarchy. That stress leads to biological changes' like the accumulation of abdominal fat, heart disease, self-destructive behaviour and (sic!) ... persistent poverty. Now, finally, we know, as endorsed and certified by distinguished scientists unsuspected of wicked sympathies and illicit connections, why some people are sunk in misery and why, unlike us, they can neither avoid sinking in it nor climb out of it once sunk. This scientific finding comes, at long last, as the much needed sweetener in the bitter reminder of our world-record inequality: the silver lining under that particularly nasty and threateningly murky cloud. It's all biology, stupid!

All the same, one would say that speaking up is admittedly better than keeping silent, and speaking up late is admittedly better than never... And a truncated, sanitised and blunted message is better than none – so one would be tempted to add. But is it indeed? Shouldn't we rather, for the sake of the message we carry and the good it was meant to accomplish, beware surrendering to that temptation?

The vision of the toxins of inequality neutralised, made liveable-with and rendered harmless by the education-driven upward mobility, and yet more disastrously, the vision of education able to keep upward social mobility in operation, begin to simultaneously evaporate. Their dissipation spells trouble to education as we know it. But it also spells trouble to the excuse favoured and commonly used is our society in the efforts to justify its injustices.

8

ON DYSFUNCTIONALITY OF THE
GLOBAL ELITES

27 April 2011

Sergei Magaril, teaching at Moscow University of Humanities, published (in the 9ᵗʰ February 2011 issue of the *Nezavisimaya Gazeta*) an article under the title 'In Search of Social Quality', which starts from a quotation from Ivan Pavlov, the first Russian Nobel laureate: 'The fate of nations is determined by the minds of their intelligentsia'. In full agreement with that opinion, Magaril proceeds to charge Russian/Soviet/Russian intellectual elites with having caused, by design or by default, the catastrophes that led to the collapse of two successive Russian state regimes, and preparing now the collapse of the third.

Magaril found an early (jotted down in 1862) proclamation of *Young Russia*, the embryo of the violent dissidence bound to rise, spread and flourish through the following half a century – spelling out, in a fit of prophetic illumination, the strikingly detailed scenario of events leading to the imminent collapse of the 300 years old Russian Empire. But, he says, that early warning that with a truly uncanny fore-sight signalled the fall of the Russian statehood came virtu-ally unnoted, and at any rate ignored; hardly anyone among the Russian ruling elite took the trouble to ponder the message, let alone to do anything to prevent its words turning flesh.

The story, he adds, repeated itself in the case of the Soviet successor to the Tsarist empire; that successor, just like the regime that preceded its coming, was destined to implode rather than explode; both regimes committed the same mortal error when focusing on the outside threat while playing down the rising temperature of social conflicts inside and the menaces emanating from its own malfunctions and ineptitude. True, the Tsarist empire suffered reverses on the war front – yet it was ultimately the internal tensions and the resulting loss of authority and capacity to act, not the enemy on the other side of the border, that sealed the fate of both empires. According to Aleksey Arbatov, the head of the Centre for International Security at the Russian Academy of Science, at the moment of its collapse the Soviet Union had at its disposal an army of four million armed men, 30 odd thousands of nuclear rocket heads, 60 thousand tanks and almost 200 atomic submarines – and no significant, pugnacious enemy at the gates.

Magaril believes that dry-rot-style deterioration is the fate of Russian statehood, the current one being no excep-tion. And as the grooves dig deeper and the trajectory gets smoother with each successive passage, repetitions of the doom scenario tend to take ever less time. The Tsarist empire took 300 years to fall apart, for the Soviet Union 74 years was enough – while a mere 19 years, Magaril muses, have passed thus far since its implosion and replacement by the current formation, but one is already tempted to wonder whether another end is nigh.

Two tribes

Precedents differ from each other and from the current variety of the Russian regime in quite a few important aspects; and yet one feature, in Magaril's opinion, repeats itself with a dull and deadly regularity: an impassable cleavage separating the worlds inhabited, respectively, by the elite and the masses. The Russian elite feels fully safe-guarded wallowing as it is in the excess of material goods and provision – whereas the masses suffer from their perpetual insufficiency. Not just economic division results, but mental split and the nearly total break of communica-tion. The two sides are less and less able to understand each other – which makes a social compact implausible and unfeasible. The sides drift in opposite directions, each inca-pable of, while uninterested in or un-hoping for, a mean-ingful coordination of their movements. According to a most recent polling, more than 90 percent of the Russian population refuses to believe in the possibility of influ-encing the state authorities' actions, whereas more than 80 percent renounces all and any responsibility for the goings-on in the country. Little wonder, then, that when listing their parental duties only one percent of respondents name the inculcation of democratic values whereas only 7 percent name the implantation of the spirit of citizenship.

In his devastating vivisection of the post-communist Russian governance, Zhan Toshchenko accuses the Russian ruling oligarchy of a 'gigantic plunder of the nation/state assets', resulting in just 22 oligarchs commanding 40 percent of nation's wealth. 'Official policy', he writes, 'and realities as well as public opinion do not just contradict each other, but point in opposite directions'. No wonder again, that among the respondents of the country-wide opinion survey 40 percent answered 'big capital', only 3 percent 'The Duma (Parliament) of the country', and a mere one percent 'people', to the question 'who holds real power in Russia'. Both quoted authors would agree that the 'people' in post-communist Russia have been demoted to the rank of state-subjects more reminiscent of serfs than of citizens. As the serfs of bygone times, the nominal citizens of 21st century Russia are treated by the ruling elite as (in Magaril's words) 'impotent, stripped of rights, socially incompetent creatures'. The incumbents of the ministerial offices and the people look at each other (if they stoop to looking, that is) as foreign nations.

Braudel's rule

Numerous Russian authors (notably Vladislav Inozemtsev in his numerous publications) expose the ever more intimate interpenetration and intertwining of oligarchic business interests with the thoroughly corrupted, self-centred, rapacious and bribes-greedy state bureaucracy (whose avarice costs the country about $240 billion annually, by conservative estimate). This, one can argue, is Russian specifity. Russian capitalism gestating under Tsarist rule was from the beginning deficient and remained crippled, passing over to the Soviet polity a misshapen heritage. Fernand Braudel is remembered for convincingly demonstrating that before the ubiquitous and eternal human appetite for lucre oriented towards instant and on-the-spot gain, while oblivious to its long-term consequences, could be transmogrified and re-shaped (as described by Max

Weber) into modern, rational, institutionalised and systemic capitalism – certain social types needed to be shaped-up and established: among others, an incorruptible judge, honest trader, disinterested public activist and craftsman imbued with the workmanship instinct. If not preceded by them, inheriting them and taking them over from the pre-capitalist conditions it is bent on eradicating, capitalism is neither able to create them and entrench on its own, nor to compensate for their absence; the case of Russia is a foremost evidence corroborating Braudel's rule.

In this undoubtedly important respect, Russia is a case of its own; facile extrapolation from its predicament to a general, all-planetary rule is for that reason ill-advised. And yet there is a common feature between the agonies gone through by the present-day Russia and the troubles confronted by quite a few other contemporary polities, including the more historically fortunate – such as followed the routes recognised by Braudel as 'normal', as much as right and proper. Today's Russia is far from being alone in experiencing the widening gap between preoccupations of the governments of the country and the worries and daily survival or 'stay-on-surface' struggles that occupy the minds, pain the hearts, and exhaust the energy while sapping the stamina of a majority of their subjects. Not in Russia alone the trust of the population in their governments being able, willing and intending to protect them, is reaching these days its historical lows.

Cracking and rotting

The crisis of political institutions inherited from the territory/nation/state trinity of the 'solid-modern' era has structural foundations: those institutions, local as they are bound to be by the verdict of history, are singularly ineffective in coping with the challenges and menaces of the era of divorce between power (ability to do things) and politics (ability to decide in doing which things power ought to be deployed), and of negative globalisation unconstrained/un-complemented by its 'positive' counterpart. Materially and spiritually 'global' elites, liberated from the confinements of places and free to move to greener grasses, have no good reasons to care about the future of the materially and spiritually 'local' populations of the places from which they happen to suck their powers at the moment, and even less reason to consider investing in that future to be their prime task and prime interest.

In a recent *NYT*, David Brooks reports the mood of the large majority of Americans – a majority as large as the majority of Russians sharing that mood. He does it under a saying-it-all title: 'The Big Disconnect':

> The current arrangements are stagnant but also fragile. American politics is like a boxing match atop a platform. Once you're on the platform, everything looks normal. But when you step back, you see that the beams and pillars supporting the platform are cracking and rotting.
>
> This cracking and rotting is originally caused by a series of structural problems that transcend any economic cycle: There are structural problems in the economy as growth slows and middle-class incomes stagnate. There are structural problems in the welfare state as baby boomers spend lavishly on themselves and impose horrendous costs on future generations. There are structural problems in energy markets as the rise of China and chronic instability in the Middle East leads to volatile

gas prices. There are structural problems with immigration policy and tax policy and on and on.

'As these problems have gone un-addressed', Brooks points out, 'Americans have lost faith in the credibility of their political system'. That faith being the prime resource upon which the whole regime rests and on which it relies for its survival, 'this loss of faith has contributed to a complex but dark national mood. The country is anxious, pessimistic, ashamed, helpless and defensive.'

The amount of Americans believing that 'the government is doing the right things' has fallen already to its historical low and nothing augurs that it may stop falling yet further in foreseeable future – as boisterous announcements of the end of crisis and impending recovery, coming from the corridors of power, have ceased to exert visible effect on the nation's mood – simply for being un-trusted as well as sounding as if coming from alien, exotic and fanciful lands. 'Seventy percent of Americans think the country is on the wrong track, according to a *The New York Times*/CBS News poll. Nearly two-thirds believe the nation is in decline, according to a variety of surveys'.

It is debatable and bound to remain so whether lessons of history may offer recipes on how to proceed in times of crises. But it is hardly questionable that those lessons may, and should, be scrutinised attentively, if the repetition of crises is to be avoided. Blindness does not exonerate the sin of oblivion.

9

ON THE UNCLASS OF PRECARIANS

14 June 2011

It has been, as far as I know, the economist Professor Guy Standing who (hitting the bull's eye!) coined the term 'precariat' to replace, simultaneously, the terms 'proletariat' and 'middle class' – both well beyond their use-by date, fully and truly 'zombie terms', as Ulrich Beck would have undoubtedly classified them. As a blogger hiding under the pen name 'Ageing Baby Boomer' suggests,

> it is the market that defines our choices and isolates us, ensuring that none of us questions how those choices are defined. Make the wrong choices and you will be punished. But what makes it so savage is that it takes no account of how some people are much better equipped than others – have the social capital, knowledge or financial resources – in order to make good choices.

What 'unites' the precariat, integrating that exceedingly

variegated aggregate into a cohesive category, is the condition of extreme disintegration, pulverisation, atomisation. Whatever their provenance or denomination, all precarians suffer – and each suffers alone, each individual suffering being well-deserved individual punishment for individually committed sins of insufficient shrewdness and deficit of industry. Individually borne sufferings are all strikingly similar: whether induced by a growing pile of utility bills and college fee invoices, miserliness of wages topped up by the fragility of available jobs and inaccessibility of solid and reliable ones, fogginess of longer-term life prospects, restless spectre of redundancy and/or demotion – they all boil down to *existential uncertainty*: that awesome blend of ignorance and impotence, and inexhaustible source of humiliation.

Such sufferings don't add up: they divide and separate the sufferers. They deny commonality of fate. They render calls to solidarity sound ludicrous. Precarians may envy or fear each other; sometimes they may pity, or even (though not too often) like one another. Few of them if any, however, would ever *respect* another creature 'like him' (or her). Indeed, why should s/he? Being 'like' I am myself, those other people must be as unworthy of respect as I am and deserve as much contempt and derision as I do! Precarians have good reason to refuse respect to other precarians and not to expect being respected by them in turn: their miserable and painful condition is an indelible trace and a vivid evidence of inferiority and indignity. That condition, all-too-visible however carefully swept under the carpet, testifies that those in authority, people who have the power to allow or to refuse rights, have refused to grant them the rights due to other, 'normal', and so respectable, humans. And so it testifies, by proxy, to the humiliation and self-contempt that inevitably follow social endorsement of personal unworthiness and ignominy.

Them and us

The prime meaning of being 'precarious' is, according to the OED, to be 'held by the favour and at the pleasure of another; hence, uncertain'. The uncertainty dubbed 'precariousness' conveys preordained and predetermined asymmetry of power to act: *they* can, *we* can't. And it's by *their* grace that we go on living: yet the grace may be withdrawn at short notice or without notice, and it's not in our power to prevent its withdrawal or even mitigate its threat. After all, *we* depend on that grace for our livelihood, whereas *they* would easily, and with much more comfort and much less worry, go on living had we disappeared from their view altogether.

Originally, the idea of 'precariousness' was a gloss over the plight and living experience of the large echelons of hangers-on, boarders and other parasites crowding around the princely and lordly kitchens. It is on the whim of the princes, lords of the manor and other high and mighty like them that their daily bread depended. The boarders owed their hosts/benefactors sycophancy and amusement; nothing was owed to them by their hosts. Those hosts, unlike their present-day successors, had names and fixed addresses. They since have lost (got free from?) both. The owners of the exquisitely frail and mobile tables at which contemporary precarians are occasionally allowed to sit are summarily called by abstract names like 'labour markets', 'economic prosperity/depression cycle', or 'global forces'.

Unlike their liquid-modern descendants a century later, contemporaries of Henry Ford Sr., Morgan, or Rockefeller were denied the ultimate 'insecurity weapon' and so unable to recycle the proletariat into precariat. The choice to move their wealth to other places – places teeming with people ready to suffer without murmur any, however cruel, factory regime, in exchange for any, however miserable, living wage – was not available to them. Just as their factory hands, their capital was 'fixed' to the place: it was sunk in heavy and bulky machinery and locked inside tall factory walls. That the dependence was for those reasons *mutual*, and that the two sides were therefore bound to stay together for a long, very long time to come, was a public secret of which both sides were acutely aware.

Limits to inequality

Confronted with such tight interdependence of such a long life-expectancy, both sides had to come sooner or later to the conclusion that it is in their interest to elaborate, nego-tiate and observe a *modus vivendi* – that is a mode of coexis-tence which will include voluntary acceptance of unavoidable limits to their own freedom of manoeuvre and the distance to which the other side in the conflict of inter-ests could and should be pushed. Exclusion was off limits, and so was indifference to misery and denial of rights. The sole alternative open to Henry Ford and the swelling ranks of his admirers, followers and imitators would have been tantamount to cutting the branch on which they were willy-nilly perched, to which they were tied just as their labourers were to their workbenches, and from which they could not move to more comfortable and inviting places. Trans-gressing the limits set by interdependence would mean destruction of the sources of their own enrichment; or fast exhausting the fertility of the soil on which their riches have grown and hoped to grow on, year in year out, in the future – perhaps forever. To put it in a nutshell: there were limits to inequality which capital could survive... Both sides of the conflict had vested interests in preventing inequality from running out of control. And each side had vested interests in keeping the other in the game.

There were, in other words, 'natural' limits to inequality and 'natural' barriers to social exclusion; the main causes of Karl Marx's prophecy of the 'proletariat's absolute pauperisation' turning self-refuting and getting sour, and the main reasons for the introduction of the social state, a state taking care of keeping labour in a condition of readiness for employment, to become a 'beyond left and right': a non-partisan issue. Also the reasons for the state needing to protect the capitalist order against the suicidal consequences of leaving unbridled the capitalists' morbid predilections, their fast-profit-seeking rapacity – and acting on that need by introducing minimum wages or time limits to the working day and week, as well as by legal protection of labour unions and other weapons of workers' self-defence.

And these were the reasons for the widening of the gap separating the rich and the poor to be halted, or even, as one would say today deploying the current idiom, 'turned negative'. To survive, inequality needed to invent the art of self-limitation. And it did – and practiced it, even if in fits and starts, for more than a century. All in all, those factors contributed to at least a partial reversal of the trend: to the mitigation of the degree of uncertainty haunting the subordinate classes and thereby to the relative levelling-up of the strength and chances of the sides engaged in the uncertainty game.

Those factors are now, ever more conspicuously, absent.

Proletariat is turning, and fast, into precariat, accompanied by fast expanding chunks of the middle classes. Reversal of this reincarnation is not on the cards. Reshaping the proletariat of yore into a fighting class was heavily power assisted – just as is, in the present-day, the atomisation of precariat, its descendant and negation.

10

ON THE FUTURE OF MIGRANTS – AND OF EUROPE

13 May 2011

'Europe needs immigrants' – former Italian Prime Minister Massimo D'Alema stated bluntly in the 10th May *Le Monde* – in direct dispute with 'the two most active European pyromaniacs', Berlusconi and Sarkozy. Calculation to support that postulate could hardly be simpler: there are today 333 million Europeans, but with the present (and still falling) average birth rate, this number will shrink to 242 million in the next 40 years.

To fill that gap, at least 30 million newcomers will be needed – otherwise our European economy will collapse together with our cherished standard of living. 'Immigrants are an asset, not a danger' – D'Alema concluded. And so is the process of cultural *métissage* ('hybridisation'), which the influx of newcomers is bound to trigger; mixing of cultural inspirations is the source of enrichment and an engine of creativity – for European civilisation as much as for any other. All the same, there is but a thin line separating enrichment from the loss of cultural identity; to prevent the cohabitation between autochthons and allochthons from eroding cultural heritages, it needs to be based therefore on respecting the principles underlying the European 'social contract'. The point is, by both sides!

Our new Europeans

How can one secure such respect, though, if recognition of social and civil rights of 'new Europeans' is so stingily and haltingly offered, and proceeds at such a sluggish pace? The immigrants, for instance, contribute currently II percent to Italian GNP, having however no right to vote in Italian elections. In addition, no one can be truly certain how large is the number of newcomers with no papers or with counterfeit documents who actively contribute to the national product and thus to the nation's wellbeing.

'How can the European Union', asks D'Alema all but rhetorically, 'permit such a situation, in which political, economic and social rights are denied to a substantive part of the population, without undermining our democratic principles?' And citizen duties coming, again in principle, in a package deal with citizen rights, can one seriously expect the newcomers to embrace, respect, support and defend those 'principles underlying the European social contract'?

Our politicians muster electoral support by blaming the immigrants for their genuine or putative reluctance to 'integrate' with the autochthon standards – while doing all they can, and promising to do yet more, to put those standards beyond the allochthons' reach. On the way, they discredit or erode the very standards which they claim to be protecting against foreign invasion.

The big question, one likely do determine the future of

Europe more than any other quandary, is which of the two contending 'facts of the matter' will eventually (yet without too much of delay) come out on top: the life-saving role played by immigrants in the fast ageing Europe few if any politicians dare so far to embroider on their banners, or the power-abetted and power-assisted rise in xenophobic sentiments eagerly recycled into electoral capital?

After their dazzling victory in the provincial election in *Baden-Württemberg*, leaving the social democrats trailing behind and putting for the first time in the history of *Bundesrepublik* one of their own, Winfried Kretschmann, at the head of a provincial government, German Greens, and notably Daniel Cohn-Bendit, begin to ponder the possibility of the German Chancellery turning green as soon as in 2013.

But who will make that history in their name? Cohn-Bendit has little doubt: Cem Ozdemir. Their present-day sharp-minded and clear-headed, dynamic, widely admired and revered co-leader, re-elected a few months ago by 88% of the votes. Until his 18th birthday, Ozdemir held a Turkish passport; then he, a young man already deeply engaged in German and European politics, selected German citizenship because of the harassments to which Turkish nationals were bound to be exposed whenever trying to enter the United Kingdom or hop over the border into neighbouring France.

One wonders: who are, in Europe's present, the advanced messengers of Europe's future? Europe's most active pair of pyromaniacs, or Daniel Cohn-Bendit?

11

ON NEVER BEING ALONE AGAIN

28 June 2011

Two apparently unconnected items of news appeared on the same day, 19th June – though one can be forgiven for overlooking their appearance... Like any news, they arrived floating in an 'information tsunami' – just two tiny drops in a flood of news meant/hoped to do the job of enlightening and clarifying while serving that of obscuring and befuddling.

One item, authored by Elisabeth Bumiller and Thom Shanker, informed of the spectacular rise in the number of drones reduced to the size of a dragonfly, or of a humming-bird comfortably perching on windowsills; both designed, in the juicy expression of Greg Parker, an aerospace engineer, 'to hide in plain sight'. The second, penned down by Brian Shelter, proclaimed the internet to be 'the place where anonymity dies'. The two messages spoke in unison, they both augured/portended the end of invisibility and autonomy, the two defining attributes of privacy – even if each of the two items was composed independently of the other and without awareness of the other's existence.

The unmanned drones, performing the spying/striking tasks for which the 'Predators' have become notorious ('More than 1900 insurgents in Pakistan's tribal areas have been killed by American drones since 2006') are about to be shrunk to the size of birds, but preferably insects (the flapping of insects' wings is ostensibly much easier to technologically imitate than the movements of birds' wings), and the exquisite aerodynamic skills of the hawk moth, an insect known for its hovering skills, have been, according to Major Michael L. Anderson, a doctoral student in advanced navigation technology, selected as a not-yet-attained, but certain to be soon reached target of the present designing flurry – because of its potential to leave far behind everything 'what our clumsy aircraft can do'.

Invisible wars

The new generation of drones will stay invisible while making everything else accessible to view; they will stay immune while rendering everything else vulnerable. In the words of Peter Baker, an ethics professor at the United States Naval Academy, those drones will usher wars in the 'post-heroic age'; but they will also, according to other 'military ethicists', push yet wider the already vast 'disconnect between the American public and its war'; they will perform, in other words, another leap (second after the substitution of the conscript by a professional army) towards making the war itself all but invisible to the nation in whose name the war is waged (no native lives will be at risk) and so that much easier – indeed so much more tempting – to conduct, thanks to the almost complete absence of collateral damages and political costs.

The next generation drones will see all while staying comfortably invisible – literally as well as metaphorically. Against being spied on, there will be no shelter – and for no one. Even the technicians who send drones into action will renounce control over their movements and so become unable, however strongly pressed, to exempt any object from the chance of falling under surveillance: the 'new and improved' drones will be programmed to fly on their own – following itineraries of their own choice in times of their own choice. The sky's the limit for the information they will supply once they are put in operation in planned numbers.

This is, as a matter of fact, the aspect of the new spying/surveilling technology armed with the capacities of acting-at-distance and autonomously, that worries most its designers and so also the two news-writers reporting their preoccupations: a 'tsunami of data', already overflowing the staff of the Air Force headquarters and threatening to run out of their digesting/absorbing powers, and thus also out of their (or anybody for that matter) control.

Since 9/11, the number of hours which Air Force employees need in order to recycle the intelligence supplied by the drones went up by 3100 percent – and each day 1500 more hours of videos and 1500 more images are added to the volume of information clamouring to be processed. Once the limited 'soda straw' view of drone sensors is replaced with a 'Gorgon Stare' able to embrace a whole city in one go (also an imminent development), 2000 analysts will be required to cope with the feeds of but one drone, instead of 19 doing such a job today. But that only means, let me comment, that fishing an 'interesting', 'relevant' object out of the bottomless container of 'data' will take some hard work and cost rather a lot of money; not that any of the potentially interesting objects may insure oneself against falling into that container in the first place. No one would ever know when the humming bird lands on his or her windowsill.

Public privacy

As for the 'death of anonymity' courtesy of the Internet, the story is slightly different: we submit our rights to privacy to slaughter on our own will. Or perhaps we just consent to the loss of privacy as a reasonable price for the wonders offered in exchange. Or the pressure to deliver our personal autonomy to the slaughterhouse is so overwhelming, so close to the condition of a flock of sheep, that only few exceptionally rebellious, bold, pugnacious and resolute wills would earnestly attempt to withstand it. One way or the other, we are, however, offered, at least nominally, a choice, as well as a semblance at least of a two-way contract, and at least a formal right to protest and sue in case of its breach: something that in the case of drones is never given.

All the same: once we are in, we stay hostages to fate. As Brian Stelter observes, 'the collective intelligence of the Internet's two billion users, and the digital fingerprints that so many users leave on websites, combine to make it more and more likely that every embarrassing video, every intimate photo, and every indelicate e-mail is attributed to its source, whether that source wants it to be or not'. It took Rich Lam, a freelance photographer taking pictures of street riots in Vancouver, just one day to trace and identify a couple caught (by accident) passionately kissing on one of his photos.

Everything private is now done, potentially, in public –

and is potentially available to public consumption; and remains available for the duration, 'till the end of time', as the Internet 'can't be made to forget' anything once recorded on any of its innumerable servers. 'This erosion of anonymity is a product of pervasive social media services, cheap cell phone cameras, free photo and video web-hosts, and perhaps most important of all, a change in people's views about what ought to be public and what ought to be private'. And let me add: the choice between the public and the private is slipping out of people's hands, with the people's enthusiastic cooperation and deafening applause. A present-day Etienne de la Boétie would be probably tempted to speak not of voluntary, but a DIY servitude...

12

ON CONSUMERISM COMING HOME TO ROOST

9 August 2011

The London riots are not hunger or bread riots. These are riots of defective and disqualified consumers. Revolutions are not staple products of social inequality; but minefields are. Minefields are areas filled with randomly scattered explosives: one can be pretty sure that some of them, some time, will explode – but one can't say with any degree of certainty which ones and when. Social revolutions being focused and targeted affairs, one can possibly do something to locate and defuse them in time. Not the minefield-type explosions, though.

In case of the minefields laid out by soldiers of one army you can send other soldiers, from another army, to dig mines out and disarm them; a dangerous job, if there ever was one – as the old soldiery wisdom keeps reminding: 'the sapper errs only once'. But in the case of minefields laid out by social inequality even such a remedy, however treacherous, is unavailable: putting the mines in and digging them up needs to be done by the same army which neither can stop adding new mines to the old nor avoid stepping on them – over and over again. Laying mines and falling victim of their explosions come in a package deal.

All varieties of social inequality derive from the division between the haves and the have-nots, as Miguel Cervantes de Saavedra noted already half a millennium ago. But in different times having or not having of *different* objects is, respectively, the states most passionately desired and most passionately resented. Two centuries ago in Europe, a few decades ago still in many some distant from Europe places, and to this day in some battlegrounds of tribal wars or playgrounds of dictatorships, the prime object setting the have-nots and the haves in conflict was bread or rice. Thank God, science, technology and certain reasonable political expedients, this is no longer the case. Which does not mean though that the old division is dead and buried. Quite the contrary... The objects of desire, whose absence is most violently resented, are nowadays many and varied – and their numbers, as well as the temptation to have them, grow by the day. And so grows the wrath, humiliation, spite and grudge aroused by *not* having them – as well as the urge to destroy what you can't have. Looting shops and setting them on fire derive from the same impulsion and gratify the same longing.

Sweet objects of desire

We are all consumers now, consumers first and foremost, consumers by right and by duty. The day after the 9/11 outrage George W. Bush, when calling Americans to get over the trauma and go back to normal, found no better words than 'go back shopping'. It is the level of our shopping activity and the ease with which we dispose of one object of consumption in order to replace it with a 'new and improved' one which serves us as the prime measure of our social standing and the score in the life-success competition. To all problems we encounter on the road away from trouble and towards satisfaction we seek solutions in shops.

From cradle to coffin we are trained and drilled to treat shops as pharmacies filled with drugs to cure or at least mitigate all illnesses and afflictions of our lives and lives in common. Shops and shopping acquire thereby a fully and truly eschatological dimension. Supermarkets, as George Ritzer famously put it, are our temples; and so, I may add, the shopping lists are our breviaries, while strolls along the shopping malls become our pilgrimages. Buying on impulse and getting rid of possessions no longer sufficiently attractive in order to put more attractive ones in their place are our most enthusing emotions. The fullness of consumer enjoyment means fullness of life. I shop, therefore I am. To shop or not to shop, this is the question.

For defective consumers, those contemporary have-nots, non-shopping is the jarring and festering stigma of a life unfulfilled – and of one's own nonentity and good-for-nothingness. Not just the absence of pleasure: absence of human dignity. Of life meaning. Ultimately, of humanity and any other ground for self-respect and respect of the others around.

Supermarkets may be temples of worship for the members of the congregation. For the anathematised, found wanting and banished by the Church of Consumers, they are the outposts of the enemy erected on the land of their exile. Those heavily guarded ramparts bar access to the goods which protect others from a similar fate: as George W. Bush would have to agree, they bar return (and for the youngsters who never yet sat on a pew, the access) to 'normality'. Steel gratings and blinds, CCTV cameras, security guards at the entry and hidden inside only add to the atmosphere of a battlefield and on-going hostilities. Those armed and closely watched citadels of enemy-in-our-midst serve as a day in, day out reminder of the natives' misery, low worth, humiliation. Defiant in their haughty and arrogant inaccessibility, they seem to shout: I dare you! But dare you what?

13

ON THE NATURE OF CAPITALISM

17 October 2011

The news of capitalism's demise is (to borrow from Mark Twain) somewhat exaggerated. Capitalism has an in-built wondrous capacity for resurrection and regeneration; though this is capacity of a kind shared with parasites – organisms that feed on other organisms, belonging to other species. After a complete or near-complete exhaustion of one host organism, a parasite tends and manages to find another, that would supply it with life juices for a successive, albeit also limited, stretch of time.

A hundred years ago Rosa Luxemburg grasped that secret of the eerie, Phoenix-like ability of capitalism to rise, repeatedly, from the ashes; an ability which leaves behind a track of devastation – the history of capitalism is marked by the graves of living organisms sucked of their life juices to exhaustion. Luxemburg, however, confined the set of organisms, lined up for the outstanding visits of the parasite, to 'pre-capitalist economies' – whose number was limited and steadily shrinking under the impact of the ongoing imperialist expansion.

With each successive visit, another one of those remaining 'virgin lands' was converted into a grazing field for capitalist exploitation, and therefore sooner rather than later made unfit for the needs of capitalist 'extended reproduction' since no longer promising the profits such an expansion required. Thinking along these lines (a fully understandable inclination, given the mostly territorial, extensive rather than intensive, lateral rather than vertical, nature of that expansion a hundred years ago), Luxemburg could not but anticipate the natural limits to the conceivable duration of the capitalist system: once all 'virgin lands' of the globe are conquered and drawn onto the treadmill of capitalist recycling, the absence of new lands for exploitation will portend and eventually enforce the collapse of the system. The parasite will die because of the absence of not-yet-exhausted organisms to feed on.

Gorging on the feast

Today capitalism has already reached the global dimension, or at any rate has come very close to reaching it – a feat which for Luxemburg was still a somewhat distant prospect. Is therefore Luxemburg's prediction close to fulfilment? I do not think it is. What has happened in the last half a century or so is capitalism learning the previously unknown and unimagined art of producing ever new 'virgin lands', instead of limiting its rapacity to the set of the already existing ones. That new art, made possible by the shift from the 'society of producers' to the 'society of consumers', and from the meeting of capital and labour to the meeting of commodity and client as the principal source of 'added value', profit and accumulation consists mostly in the progressive commodification of life functions, market mediation in successive needs' satisfaction, and substituting desire for need in the role of the fly-wheel of the profit-aimed economy.

The current crisis derives from the exhaustion of an artificially created virgin land; one built out of the millions stuck in the 'culture of saving books' instead of 'culture of credit cards'; in other words, out of the millions of people too shy to spend the yet-unearned money, living on credit, taking loans and paying interest. Exploitation of that particular 'virgin land' is now by and large over and it has been left now to the politicians to clean up the debris left by the bankers' feast; that task has been removed from the realm of bankers' responsibility into the dustbin of 'political problems' and recast belatedly from an economic issue into the question of (to quote Chancellor Merkel) 'political will'. But one is entitled to surmise that in myriad offices of capitalism hard labour is currently focused on constructing new 'virgin lands' – though also burdened with the curse of fairly limited life-expectancy, given the parasitic nature of capitalism.

Capitalism proceeds through creative destruction. What is created is capitalism in a 'new and improved' form – and what is destroyed is self-sustaining capacity, livelihood and dignity of its innumerable and multiplied 'host organisms' into which all of us are drawn/seduced one way or another. I suspect that one of capitalism's crucial assets derives from the fact that the imagination of economists, including its critics, lags well behind its own inventiveness, arbitrariness of its undertaking and ruthlessness of the way in which it proceeds.

This column is based on an interview conducted by Fernando Duarte for O Globo.

PART II

FROM HARD FACTS TO DONALD TRUMP

14

SOFT POWER AND HARD FACTS

4 May 2012

Joseph S. Nye Jr. has turned upside down Machiavelli's infamous recommendation to the Prince: *it is safer when people fear you than when they love you...* Whether or not that recommendation was right for the Prince remains a moot question; but it no longer makes sense for presidents and prime ministers.

Nye would agree that because of its eminently flickery habits love is not particularly fit for a foundation on which long-term confidence could be built and rest; but so is, he adds, the state of being frightened – and especially if not reconfirmed by the Prince continuing to deliver on his threat to punish: to be as cruel, ruthless, bestial – and above all as indomitable and irresistible – as he pretended and/or was believed to be.

Yet more unreliable and frustrating that recommendation turns out to be, if love (complete with awe, respect, trust and readiness to forgive occasional *faux pas*, misdeeds and improprieties) is absent or not strong enough to compensate for the display of incompetence or impotence. In short: presidents and prime ministers beware - all said, *it is safer to be loved than to be feared*. If you have to resort to overt hostilities, don't measure your success by the numbers of enemies killed, but by the quantity of friends, admirers and allies you've managed to summon, acquire and/or reassure.

You don't believe this to be true? Just look at what happened to the Soviet Union, when it emerged from the battlefields of the Second World War with an astonishing capital of admiration and respect among world-wide opinion-makers – only to squander it by drowning the Hungarian uprising in rivers of blood and then crushing and strangling the Czechoslovak experiment with 'socialism with a human face', and topping up its ignominy with a disastrous economic performance and the misery produced and reproduced at home under the aegis of the planned economy.

Destroying capital - and trust

Or look at the United States of America, revered world-wide and looked up to once having emerged triumphant from two successive wars against totalitarian powers – only to fritter away an unprecedentedly huge, seemingly inexhaustible supply of trust, hope, adoration and love by invading Iraq and Afghanistan for fraudulent reasons and on false premises: whereas its weapons meant to frighten proved to be superbly effective and as murderous as one was made to expect (Saddam Hussein's awesome army was swept away in Blitzkrieg fashion, and the Taliban fortresses needing but a few days to fall apart and collapse in a manner of cardboard boxes), the US lost one by one almost all members of the initial coalition and all its potential allies in the Arab world. What does that amount to? The US killed about one hundred thousand uniformed and un-uniformed Iraqis, but lost millions of sympathisers.

'The military-manufacturing model of leadership', Nye concludes, has nowadays fallen decidedly out of fashion; perhaps the idea of leadership as we know it has followed its suit. At least this is what the spokesmen of the 'Wall Street Occupiers' insist, making merit out of an absence of leaders. Or this is what two Americans in every three, reporting their lack of trust in the powers that be, confirm. Or what the recent research commissioned by Xerox Company, and showing that success in collective undertakings depends in 42 percent of these on team work, but only in 10 percent on the quality of leaders, suggests.

People are no longer as meekly submissive as they used to be or used to be believed to be, and people are getting less prone than previously reckoned to fear punishment for disobedience. It gets tougher to coerce them into doing what the powers that be wish them to be doing. On the other hand, though, they become more amenable to be seduced as the temptations gain in their amplitude and technical sophistication. Present and future presidents and prime ministers pay note: Joseph S. Nye Jr., seasoned and battle-tested counsellor of presidents and member of many brain trusts of the highest-rank, recommends to all current and prospective power holders to rely less on *hard* power (whether military or economic), and more on its *soft* alternative/complement. All in all, on *smart* power: the golden mean of the two, an optimal mixture utterly difficult thus far to be found yet imperative to be sought with an eye on the right dose of each of the two ingredients: an ideal combination of the threat of breaking necks and the effort of winning hearts.

The end of combat

Among the military and the political elites alike, Nye's is an authoritative – widely and attentively listened to – voice. It shows a way out from the long and lengthening series of failed military adventures and only thinly masked defeats. I guess that what his voice signals/reflects is a sort of end of era: an era of wars as we knew them, wars understood as a principally symmetrical affair – a *combat*. Coercive instruments of *hard* power are by no means abandoned; nor are such weapons likely to fall out of favour and use. But they are increasingly designed with an idea of making reciprocation, and so the combat-style symmetry, all but impossible. Regular armies hardly ever meet face to face; weapons are hardly ever discharged point-blank. In terrorist activities, as much as in the 'war against terrorism' (the terminological distinction reflecting the new asymmetry of hostilities) total avoidance of direct confrontation with the enemy is attempted by both sides with growing success. On the two sides of the frontline, two starkly different strategies and tactics of hostilities develop. Each side has its own limitations – but also its advantages, to which the other side has no effective response. In the end-result, the present-day hostility replacing the combat of yesteryear consists of two unilateral blatantly asymmetrical actions, aiming at rendering the very possibility of symmetry null and void.

On one side, the tendency to reduce hostility to actions at-a-distance large enough to deny the enemy the chance to reply or indeed prevent, let alone preempt, a response in kind; such actions are conducted with the help of smart missiles or ever more sophisticated drones, difficult to locate and divert. On the other side, the tendency is towards simplification of weaponry: its reduction in costs, size and complexity of its assembly and use. The cost of hijacking a plane and using it to devastating material, yet even more disastrous psychological effects, is but a few dollars higher than the price of an air-flight ticket.

If measured by the standards of the first side, the effects tend to be disproportionately huge in proportion to expenditures; but this is not the whole story of the asymmetry of costliness. Simplicity and easy accessibility of materials from which their weapons are constructed make the detection of planned terrorists acts in their early stages, and so their prevention, exceedingly difficult; but the crucial point that follows from that is that the costs of the attempts to preempt the innumerable anticipated terrorist acts (based almost entirely on guesswork and 'playing it safe'), tend to leave far behind the costs of dealing with the damages perpetrated by the few acts already accomplished; having to be met entirely by the financial capacities of the assaulted side, they may well turn in the long term into the terrorists' most effective and most devastating weapon (just think how much does it cost to spy out, spot and confiscate day in, day out, millions of water bottles on thousands of airports around the world, just because someone, somewhere, some time had been caught or perhaps just suspected of composing a cottage-industry or home-baked bomb by mixing small quantities of two liquids).

Some people reckon that the collapse of the Soviet Union was triggered by Reagan involving Gorbachev in an arms chase the Soviet economy couldn't enter without becoming bankrupt. Watching the already exorbitant yet still fast rising federal debt of the US, one may feel excused if wondering whether Bin Laden and his successors might have managed to take a hint and learn the lesson, and are set to repeat Reagan's feat.

15

DO FACEBOOK AND TWITTER HELP SPREAD DEMOCRACY?

8 May 2012

The official American establishment's reaction to the Iranian youth venting briefly on the streets of Tehran their protest against fraudulent elections in June 2009 bore striking resemblance to a commercial campaign on behalf of the likes of Facebook, Google or Twitter. I suppose that some gallant investigative journalist, to whose company alas I do not belong, could have supplied weighty material proofs of such impression.

The *Wall Street Journal* pontificated: 'this would not happen without Twitter'! Andrew Sullivan, an influential and well-informed American blogger, pointed to Twitter as 'the critical tool for organising the resistance in Iran', whereas the venerable *New York Times* waxed lyrically, proclaiming a combat between 'thugs firing bullets' and 'protesters firing tweets'. Hillary Clinton went on record announcing in her 21st January 2010 'Internet Freedom' speech the birth of the 'samizdat of our day' and proclaiming the need 'to put these tools (meaning 'viral videos and blog post') in the hands of people around the world who will use them to advance democracy and human rights'. 'Information freedom', she opined, 'supports the peace and security that provide a foundation for global progress'. (Let me though note right away that little water had flown under Potomac bridges before the American political elite started, as if following the French injunction of *deux poids, deux mesures*, to demand restrictions on Wiki-Leaks and a prison sentence on its founder).

Ed Pilkington recalls Mark Pfeiffe, a George Bush adviser who nominated Twitter for the Nobel Prize, and quotes Jared Cohen, an official in the US State Department, who described Facebook as 'one of the most organic tools for democracy the world has ever seen'. To put it in a nutshell: Jack Dorsey, Mark Zuckerberg and their compan-ions-in-arms are the generals of the advancing Democracy-and-Human-Rights Army – and we all, tweeting and sending Facebook messages, are its soldiers. Media is indeed the message – and the message of the digital media is the 'information curtain descending' and uncovering thereby the new planet-scape of people power and universal human rights.

Social media as espionage tool

It is such un-common-sense of the American political and opinion-making elite and other unpaid salespersons of digital services that Evgeny Morozov, a 26-years young student and newcomer from Belorussia to America, berated, ridiculed, and condemned it as a 'net delusion' in the book under the same title, just published by Allen Lane. Among many other points Morozov managed to squeeze in his four-hundred-pages-long study, was that, according to Al-Jazeera, there were but 60 active Twitter accounts in Tehran, and so the organisers of the demos used mostly such shamefully old-fashioned techniques of getting attention as making telephone calls or knocking on the neighbours' doors; but that the clever rulers of autocratic Iran, no less internet-savvy than ruthless and unscrupulous, looked up on Face-book to find out the links to any known dissidents, using that information to isolate, incarcerate and disempower the potential leaders of revolt – and nip the democratic chal-lenge to autocracy (if there ever be one) in the bud. And there are many and different ways in which authoritarian regimes can use the internet to their own advantage, Morozov points out – and many of them did use them and go on using them.

To start with, social networks offer a cheaper, quicker, more thorough and altogether easier way to identify and locate the current or potential dissidents than any of the traditional instruments of surveillance. And as David Lyon argues and attempts to show in our joint study *Liquid Surveillance*, surveillance-through-social-networks is made so much more effective thanks to the cooperation of its intended objects and victims.

We live in a confessional society, promoting public self-exposure to the rank of the prime and easiest available, as well as arguably most potent and the sole truly proficient, proof of social existence. Millions of Facebook users vie with each other to disclose and put on public record the most intimate and otherwise inaccessible aspects of their identity, social connections, thoughts, feelings and activities. Social websites are fields of a voluntary, do-it-yourself form of surveillance, beating hands down (both volume-wise and expenditure-wise) the specialist agencies manned by professionals of spying and detection. A true windfall, a genuinely pennies-from-heaven-style, for every dictator and his secret services – and a superb complement to the numerous 'banoptical' institutions of democratic society concerned with preventing the unwanted and undeserving (that is, all those who behave or are likely to behave *comme il ne faut pas*) from being mistakenly admitted or worming them-selves surreptitiously into our decent self-selected democ-ratic company. One of *The Net Delusion* chapters is titled 'Why the KGB wants you to join Facebook'.

Slacktivists

Morozov spies out the many ways in which authoritarian, nay tyrannical regimes may beat the alleged freedom fighters in their own game, using the technology in which the apostles and panegyrists of the Internet's democratic bias vested their hopes. No news here; old technologies were similarly used by past dictators to pacify and disarm their victims: research showed that East Germans with access to Western television were less likely to express dissatisfaction with the regime. As to the admittedly much more potent, digital informatics, 'the Internet has provided so many cheap and easily available entertainment fixes to those living under authoritarianism that it has become considerably harder to get people to care about politics at all'. That is, unless politics is recycled into another exciting, full of sound and fury yet comfortingly toothless, safe and innocuous variety of entertainment; something practiced by the new generation of 'slacktivists', who believe that 'clicking on a Facebook petition counts as a political act' and so 'dissipate their energies on a thousand distractions', each meant for instant consumption and one-off use, which the

Internet is a master supreme of producing and disposing of daily (just one of numberless examples of how effective is the political slacktivism in changing the ways and means of the real world, is the sad case of 'Save the Children of Africa' group: it needed several years to collect the princely sum of $12,000, while the un-saved children of Africa went on dying).

With the popular mistrust of the powers-that-be spreading and deepening, and the popular esteem of the power-to-the-people potential of the Internet rising sky-high through joint efforts of Silicon Valley marketing and Hillary Clinton-style lyrics recited and broadcast from thousands of academic offices, no wonder that pro-government propaganda has a better chance of being listened to and absorbed if arriving to its targets through the Internet. The more clever among the authoritarians know this all-too-well to be the case: after all, informatics experts are all-too-available for hiring, eager to sell their services to the highest bidder.

Hugo Chavez is on Twitter and boasts allegedly half a million Facebook friends. While in China there is ostensibly a genuine army of the government-subsidised bloggers (commonly baptised 'the 50 cents party' for being paid 50 cents for every entry). Morozov keeps reminding his readers that – as Pat Kane puts it – 'patriotic service can be as much a motivation for the young socio-technical operative as the bohemian anarchism of Assange and his pals'. Info-hackers may equally enthusiastically and with the same volume of good will and sincerity join a new 'Transparency International' as a new 'Red Brigade'. The Internet would support both choices with equal equanimity.

It is an old, very old story told all over again: one can use axes to hew wood or to cut heads. The choice does not belong to axes but to those who hold them. Whatever the holders' choices, the axes won't mind. And however sharp the edges which it may be currently cutting, technology would not 'advance democracy and human rights' for (and instead of) you.

16

THE PRECARIAT IS WELCOMING GENERATION Y

22 May 2012

In Natalie Brafman's article titled *Génération Y: du concept marketing à la réalité*, published in its 19th May issue, *Le Monde* pronounced the Generation Y to be 'more individualistic and disobedient to bosses, but above all more precarious' – if compared with the 'boom' and 'X' generations that preceded it, that is.

Between themselves journalists, marketing experts and social researchers (in that order...) assembled into the imagined formation (class? category?) of 'Generation Y' young men and women between about 20 and 30 years of age (that is, born roughly between the middle of the 1980s and the middle of the 1990s). And what is becoming more obvious by the day is that the Generation Y, so composed, may have a better founded claim to the status of a culturally specific formation that is a bona fide 'generation', and so also a better justified plea for an acute attention of traders, newschasers and scholars than had its predecessors.

It is common to argue that what grounds the claim and justifies the plea is first and foremost the fact that the members of Generation Y are the first humans who have never experienced a world without Internet and know as well as practise digital communication 'in real time'. If you share in the widespread assessment of the arrival of informatics as a watershed in human history, you are obliged to view Generation Y as at least a milestone in the history of culture. And it is so viewed; and so, spied out, found and recorded. As an appetiser of sorts, Brafman suggests that the curious habit of the French to pronounce 'Y' in case it is linked to the idea of a generation in an English way – as 'why' could be explained by this being a 'questioning generation'. In other words, a formation taking nothing for granted.

Let me, however, add right away that the questions that generation is in the habit of asking are addressed by and large to the anonymous authors of Wikipedia, to Facebook pals and Twitter addicts – but neither to their parents or bosses nor 'public authorities', from whom they don't seem to expect relevant, let alone authoritative, reliable and so worth listening-to answers.

The surfeit of their questions, I guess, is like in so many other aspects of our consumerist society an offer-driven demand; with an iPhone as good as grafted onto the body there are constantly, 24 hours a day and 7 days a week, loads of answers feverishly searching for questions as well as throngs of answer-peddlers frantically seeking demand for their services. And another suspicion: do the Generation Y people spend so much time on the Internet because of having been tormented by questions they crave to be answered? Or are rather the questions which they ask once connected to the hundreds of their Facebook friends updated versions of Bronislaw Malinowski's 'phatic expressions' (as for instance 'how do you do' or 'how are you', the kind of elocutions whose only function is to perform a *sociating task*, as opposed to *conveying information*, the task being in this case to announce your presence and availability for sociating – not far from the 'small talk' conducted to break boredom, but above all to escape alienation and loneliness at a crowded party).

Precarious chat

Of the surfing of infinitely vast Internet expanses the members of Generation Y are indeed unequaled masters. And of 'being connected': they are the first generation in history measuring the number of friends (translated nowadays primarily as companions-in-connecting) in hundreds, if not thousands. And they are the first who spend most of their awake-time sociating through conversing – though not necessarily aloud, and seldom in full sentences. This all is true. But is it the whole truth of Generation Y? What about that part of the world which they, by definition, did not and could not experience, having therefore had little if any chance to learn how to encounter it point-blank, without electronic/digital mediation, and what consequences that inescapable encounter might have? The part which nonetheless pretends, and with a spectacularly formidable and utterly indismissable effect, to determine the rest of, and perhaps even the most important rest, their lives' truth?

It is that 'rest' which contains the part of the world that supplies another feature standing Generation Y apart from its predecessors: precariousness of the place they have been offered by society they are still struggling, with mixed success, to enter. 25 percent of people below 25 years of age remain unemployed. Generation Y as a whole chain up to the *CDD* (*Contrat à durée déterminée*, fixed-term contracts) and *stages* (training practices) – both shrewdly evasive and crudely, mercilessly exploitative expedients. If in 2006 there were about 600 thousand *stagiaires* in France, their current number is estimated to vacillate somewhere between 1.2 and 1.5 million. And for most, visiting that liquid-modern purgatory renamed 'training practice' is unmissable: agreeing and submitting to such expedients as *CDD* or *stages* is a necessary condition of finally reaching, at the advanced average age of 30, the possibility of a full-time, of 'infinite' duration employment.

An immediate consequence of frailty and in-built transience of social positions which the so-called 'labour market' is capable of offering is the widely signalled profound change of attitude toward the idea of 'job' – and particularly of a steady job, a job safe and reliable enough to be capable of determining the middle-term social standing and the life prospects of its performer. Generation Y is marked by the unprecedented, and growing, 'job-cynicism' of its members (and no wonder, if for instance Alexandra de Felice, reputable observer/commentator of the French labour market, expects an average member of Generation Y, if the current trends continue, to change bosses and employers 29 times in the course of their working life; though some other observers, as Rouen Business School Professor Jean Pralong, call for more realism in estimating the youngsters' chances of matching the pace of job-change to the cynicism of their job-attitudes: in a labour market in its present condition, it would take a lot of daring and courage to snap one's finger at the boss and tell him face-to-face that one would rather go than stay with such a pain in the ass.

Life elsewhere

So, according to Jean Pralong, the youngsters would rather bear with their dreary plight however off-putting that plight might be, were they allowed to stay longer in their quasi-jobs. But seldom are they, and if they are they would not know how long the stay of execution could last. One way or another, members of Generation Y differ from their predecessors by complete or almost complete absence of job-related illusions, by a lukewarm only (if any) commitment to the jobs currently held and the companies which offer them, and a firm conviction that life is elsewhere and resolution (or at least a desire) to live it elsewhere. This is indeed an attitude seldom to be found among the members of the 'boom' and 'X' generations.

Some of the bosses admit that the guilt is on their side. They are reluctant to lay the blame for the resulting disenchantment and nonchalance prevalent among young employees on the youngsters themselves. Brafman quotes Gilles Babinet, a 45 year-old entrepreneur, bewailing the dispossession of the young generation of all or nearly all autonomy their fathers had and successfully guarded – priding themselves on possessing the moral, intellectual and economic principles of which their society was presumed to be the guardian and from which it wouldn't allow its members to budge. He believes that the kind of society which Generation Y enters is on the contrary anything but seductive: if I was their age, Babinet admits, I'd behave exactly as they do.

As for the youngsters themselves, they are as blunt as their predicament is straightforward: we have not the slightest idea, they say, what tomorrow is likely to bring. The labour market closely guards their secrets – just as impenetrable fortresses do: little point in trying to peep inside, let alone attempting to break the gates open. And as to the guessing of its intentions – it's hard to believe that there are any. Tougher and more knowledgeable minds than mine are known mostly for their abominable misjudgments in the guessing game. In a hazardous world, we have no choice but being gamblers. Whether by choice, or by necessity; and it does not matter in the end by what, does it?

Well, these state-of-the-mind reports are remarkably similar to the confessions of the more thoughtful and sincere among the *precarians* – members of the *precariat*, the most rapidly growing section of our post-credit-collapse and post-certainty world. Precarians are defined by having their homes erected (complete with bedrooms and kitchens) on quicksand, and by their own self-confessed ignorance ('no idea what is going to hit me') and impotence ('even if I knew, I wouldn't have the power to divert the blow').

It has been thought until now that the appearance and formidable, some say explosive, expansion of the precariat, sucking in and incorporating more and more of the past working- and middle-classes, was a phenomenon arising from the fast changing *class* structure. It is indeed – but isn't it, in addition, also a matter of a changing *generational* structure? Of bringing forth a state of affairs in which a suggestion 'tell me the year of your birth, and I'll tell you to which social class you belong' won't sound that much fanciful at all?

17

EUROPE IS TRAPPED BETWEEN POWER AND POLITICS

14 May 2013

That the disease which brought the European Union into the intensive-care ward and has kept it there since, for quite a few years, is best diagnosed as a 'democratic deficit' is fast turning into a commonplace. Indeed, it is taken increasingly for granted and is hardly ever seriously questioned. Some observers and analysts ascribe the illness to an inborn organic defect, some others seek carriers of the disease among the personalities of the European Council and the constituencies they represent; some believe the disease has by now become terminal and beyond treatment, some others trust that a bold and harsh surgical intervention may yet save the patient from agony. But hardly anyone questions the diagnosis. All, or nearly all, agree that the roots of the malaise lie in the breakdown of communication between the holders of political offices (policy-makers in Brussels and/or the politicians of the European Council) who set the tune and the people called to follow the set score with or without being asked and offering their consent.

At least there is no deficit of arguments to support the diagnosis of the 'deficit of democracy' inside the European Union. The state of the Union, no doubt, calls for intensive care, and its future – the very chance of its survival – lies in the balance. Such a condition we call, since the ancient beginnings of medical practice, 'crisis'. The term was coined to denote precisely such a moment – in which the doctor faces the necessity of urgently deciding to which of the known and available assortment of medical expedients to resort in order to nudge the patient onto the course of convalescence. When speaking of crisis of whatever nature, including the economic, we convey firstly the feeling of *uncertainty*, of our *ignorance* of the direction in which the affairs are about to turn – and secondly the urge to intervene: to select the right measures and *decide* to apply them promptly. Describing a situation as 'critical', we mean just that: the conjunction of diagnosis and call for action. And let me add that there is a hint of endemic contradiction in such an idea: after all, the admission of the state of uncertainty/ignorance portends ill for the chance of selecting the right measures and prompting the affairs in the desired direction.

Resourceful nannies

Let's focus on the most recent *economic* crisis largely responsible for laying bare the critical state of the *political* union of Europe. The right point to start is to remember the horrors of the 1920s-1930s by which all and every one of successive issues of the economy have tended to be measured since – and ask whether the current, post credit-collapse crisis can be seen and described as their reiteration, throwing thereby some light on its likely sequel. While admitting that there are numerous striking similarities between the two crises and their manifestations (first and foremost massive and prospect-less unemployment and soaring social inequality), there is, however, one crucial difference between the two that sets them apart and renders comparing one to the other questionable, to say the least.

While horrified by the sight of markets running wild and causing fortunes together with workplaces to evaporate and while knocking off viable businesses into bankruptcy, victims of the late 1920s stock exchange collapse had little doubt as to where to look for rescue: of course to the state – to a *strong* state, so strong as to be able to force the course of affairs into obedience with its will. Opinions as to the best way out of the predicament might have differed, even drastically, but there was virtually no disagreement as to *who* was fit to tackle the challenge thanks to being sufficiently resourceful to push the affairs the way the opinion-makers eventually selected: of course *the state*, equipped with both resources indispensable for the job: *power* (ability to have things done), and *politics* (ability to decide which ones of the proposed things ought to be given priority). Alongside the overwhelming majority of the informed or intuitive opinions of the time, John Maynard Keynes put his wager on the resourcefulness of the state. His recommendations made sense in as far as the 'really existing' states could rise to such popular expectations. And indeed, the aftermath of the collapse stretched to its limits the same post-Westphalian model of a state armed with absolute and indivisible sovereignty over its territory and on everything it contains – even if in the direction as diverse as the Soviet state-managed, German state-regulated and US state-stimulated economies.

This post-Westphalian ideal type of an omnipotent territorial state emerged from war not only unscathed, but considerably expanded to match the comprehensive ambitions of a 'social state' – a state insuring all its citizens against individual misfortune (selectively striking caprices of fate) and the threat of indignity in whatever form (of poverty, negative discrimination, unemployment, homelessness, social exclusion) that haunted pre-war generations. It was also adopted, even if in a somewhat cut-down rendition, by numerous new states and quasi-states emerging amidst the ruins of colonial empires. The 'glorious thirty' years that followed the war were marked by the rising expectations that all harrowing social problems had been or were about to be resolved and left behind; and the tormenting memories of pre-war poverty and mass unemployment were about to be buried once for all.

Losing faith

Something largely unforeseen happened, however, that jostled most of the Europeans off the then selected track. In the 1970s the heretofore uninterrupted economic progress ground to a halt and was supplanted by a seemingly unstoppable rise in unemployment, seemingly unmanageable inflation and above all the growing and ever more evident inability of the states to deliver on their promise of comprehensive insurance. Gradually yet ever more starkly, states manifested their inability to deliver on their promises. Gradually, but apparently unrelentlessly, the faith and trust in the potency of the state started to erode. Functions claimed heretofore and jealously guarded by the states as their monopoly and widely considered by the public and the most influential opinion-makers and guardians of common sense as the state's inalienable obligation and mission seemed suddenly too heavy for nation states to carry. Peter Drucker famously declared that people *need*, *should* and shortly *will* abandon hopes of salvation descending 'from above' – from the state or society; the number of ears keen to absorb that message grew at accelerating pace. In the popular perception, aided and abetted by the chorus of a fast-growing part of the learned and opinion-making public, the state was degraded from the rank of the most powerful engine of universal well-being to that of a most obnoxious and annoying obstacle to economic progress and indeed efficiency of human enterprise.

Just as during the Great Depression of the 1920s-1930s, the opinion-setters as well as the widening circles of the general public deemed *to know* this time what kind of vehicles are called for to replace the extant ones, not so long ago viewed as trusty yet increasingly rusty and overdue for the scrap yard. Once more, it seemed to be obvious as well what kind of powerful force is destined, willing and able to lead the way out of the current crisis. This time, however, public trust was all but withdrawn from the political state only to be reinvested in the 'invisible hand of the market' – and indeed (as Milton Friedman, Ronald Reagan, Margaret Thatcher and the fast expanding bevy of their enthusiastic acolytes kept hammering home) it is the market ability of unerring knack for spotting profit opportunities that would accomplish what the ethics-inspired state bureaucrats abominably failed to achieve. 'Deregulation', 'privatisation', 'subsidiarisation' were to bring what regulation, nationalisation and the communal, state-guided undertakings so obviously and abominably failed to deliver. State functions had to be and were to be shifted sideways, to the market, that admittedly 'politics-free' zone, or dropped downwards, onto the shoulders of human individuals, now expected to divine individually, inspired and set in motion by their greed, what they did not manage to produce collectively, inspired and moved by communal spirit.

The 'glorious thirty' were therefore followed by the 'opulent thirty'; the years of a consumerist orgy and continuous, seemingly unstoppable growth of GNP indices all over the place. The wager put on pursuit of profits seemed to be paying off: its benefits, as later transpired, came into view much earlier than its costs. It took us a couple of dozens of years to find out what fuelled the consumerist miracle: not so much the magic 'invisible hand of the market', as the discovery by the banks and the credit card issuers of a vast virgin land open to and yelling for exploitation: a land populated by millions of people indoctrinated by the precepts of 'saving-books culture' and still in the throes of the puritan commandment to desist the temptation of spending money, particularly its unearned variety. And it took yet a few years more to awaken to the sombre truth that initially fabulous returns of investing in virgin lands must soon reach their natural limits, run out of steam and eventually stop coming altogether. When that ultimately happened, the bubble burst and the *fata morgana* of perpetual and infinitely expanding opulence vanished from view under the sky covered with dark clouds of prospect-less redundancy, bankruptcies, infinite debt-repayment, a drastic fall in living standards, the curtailing of life ambitions – and of social degradation of the upward-looking middle classes to the status of defence-less 'precariat'.

The gods that failed

Another crisis of another agency, then? A collapse of one more vehicle in which the hope of the 'economic progress' perpetuum mobile had been invested? Yes, but this time with a difference – and a fateful, seminal one. As in the previous cases, old vehicles of 'progress' appear today to be overdue for the scrap heap, but there is no promising invention in sight in which one could reinvest the hope of carrying the rudderless victims out of trouble. After the loss of public trust in the wisdom and potency of the state, the turn has come of the dexterity of the 'invisible hand of the market' to lose credibility. While almost every one of the old ways of doing things lies discredited, the new ways are – at best – on the drawing board or in early experimentation stage. No one can swear, hand on heart, to the effectiveness of any of the latter. Too well aware of the hopes that failed, we have no hopeful runners-up to bet on. Crisis being the time of deciding what way of proceeding to choose, in the arsenal of human experience there seem to be no trustworthy strategies left to choose from.

We are now painfully aware, at least for a moment and until the human, all-too-human, therapy-through-forgetting will have done its job, that if left to their own devices the profit-guided markets lead to economic and social catastrophes. But should we – and above all *could* we – return to the once deployed yet now unemployed or under-employed devices of state supervision, control, regulation and management? Whether we *should* is obviously a moot question. What is well-nigh certain, however, is that we *couldn't* –

whatever answer we choose to that question. We couldn't because the state is no longer what it used to be a hundred years ago, or what it was believed/hoped then soon to become. In its present condition, the state lacks the means and resources to perform the task which effective supervision and control of the markets, not to mention their regulation and management, required.

Trust in the state's capacity to deliver rested on the supposition that both conditions of effective management of social realities – power and politics – are in the hands of states assumed to be a sovereign (exclusive and indivisible) master within its territorial boundaries. By now, however, the state has been expropriated of a large and growing part of its past genuine or imputed power, which has been captured by the supra-state, for all practical intents exterritorial global forces operating in a politically uncontrolled 'space of flows' (Manuel Castells' term), whereas the effective reach of the extant political agencies did not progress beyond the state boundaries. Which means, purely and simply, that finance, investment capital, labour markets or circulation of commodities are beyond the remit and reach of the only political agencies currently available to do the job of supervision and regulation. It is the politics chronically afflicted with the deficit of power (and so also of coercion) that confronts the challenge of powers emancipated from political control.

Absent agent

To cut the long story short: the present crisis differs from its historical precedents in as far as it is lived through in the situation of a *divorce between power and politics*. That divorce results in the absence of any agency able to do what every 'crisis' by definition requires: choose the way to proceed and apply the therapy which that choice calls for. The absence, it looks, will continue to paralyse the search for a viable solution until power and politics, now in the state of divorce, are re-married. It also looks, however, that under conditions of global interdependence such a remarriage is hardly conceivable inside one state, however large and resourceful; or even inside an aggregate of states, as long as power is free to abandon at will and without notice any territory politically monitored and controlled by political units clutching to the ghosts of post-Westphalian illusions. It looks like we are facing now the awesome yet imperative task of raising politics and its institutions to the global level, on which large part of effective power to have things done already resides. All pressures, from brutally mundane to sublimely philosophical, whether derived from survival interests or dictated by ethical duty, tend to point nowadays in the same direction – however little we have thus far advanced on the road leading there. Inside the European Union, *a half-way inn on that road*, those pressures feel more severe and pain more than in any other area of the globalised planet.

Deficit of democracy is by no means a unique affliction of the European Union. Every single democratic state – every political body that aims or pretends to a full sovereign rule over its territory in the name of its citizens and not by the will of a Machiavellian Prince or Schmittian *Führer* – finds itself currently *in a double bind*, exposed to the pressures of extraterritorial powers immune to the political will and demands of the citizenship, which it can't at any rate meet due to its chronic deficit of power. With power and politics subject to separate and mutually autonomous sets of interests, and state governments tussling between two pressures impossible to reconcile, trust in the ability and will of the political establishment to deliver on its promise is fast fading, whereas communication between ruling elites and the *hoi polloi* lies all but broken; election after election, electors are guided by the frustration of their past hopes invested in the currently ruling team – rather than by their preference for a specific policy, or commitment and loyalty to a specific sector in the spectrum of ideologies.

A love-hate relationship

The European Union, as an aggregate of nation states charged statutorily with the replacement of an inter-state competition with cooperation and sharing, finds itself in a truly unenviable plight: a need to assume an incongruous mix of mutually incompatible roles – of a protective shield or a lightning rod intercepting and arresting, or at least attenuating, the impact of powers freely roaming the global 'space of flows' and of an enforcer pressing its member states to absorb the remainder of the force of impact that resisted interception and managed to break in through the outer circle of trenches. No wonder that the attitudes of the member states' populations to the Union's policies tend to be and to stay ambivalent, vacillating between the extremes of *Hass* and *Liebe*: an attitude mirroring the persistent ambivalence of the two-in-one role which the Union is bound to play more by the stark necessity it cannot control than by a choice it is free to make.

There is little doubt that there is much room yearning for reform and improvement in the Union's ailing structures struggling for a modicum of coherence under the condition of unmitigated ambivalence. There is, however, only so much which the most ingenious reforms can achieve as long as they are considered and handled as a solely internal

European affair. The roots of Europe's problems – dis-coordination of power and politics brought about by a globality of powers confronting locally confided and territorially constricted politics – lie far beyond Europe's control. The problems Europe faces can be alleviated but can hardly be fully resolved and prevented from rebounding unless the power and politics presently separated and in the state of divorce are brought back into wedlock and forced to work in tandem.

And so, in the case of badly needed and urgently demanded constitutional adjustment, quick fixes – let alone ultimate and lasting solutions to the current problems – are unlikely to be found and put in place. Whatever else the sought-after reform of the Union will be, it can't be a one-off deed, but only a process of perpetual reinvention. This is the 'hard fact' reality we have little choice but to accept and consider in our thoughts and actions.

And there is something else we need to consider and focus our thoughts and actions on. Whether we are aware of it or not, and whether by design or by default, the European Union is a laboratory (if not unique, then surely the currently most advanced on a global scale) in which ways to deal with the outcomes of present dis-coordination of power and politics are designed, explored and put to tests. This is, arguably, the most important and consequential among Europe's current contributions to the condition and prospects of the planet; indeed, to its chances of survival. Europe's present quandary anticipates the challenges which the rest of the planet – the whole of the planet and all of its inhabitants – are bound, sooner or later, to experience first-hand, face up to and live through. Our present pains may yet (are destined to?) prove to be the birth pangs of a humanity at peace with itself and drawing proper conclusions from the demands of its new – irreversibly globalised – condition. What presently feels like an unbearably hurtful squeeze of a vice may yet be found in retrospect to have been severe, yet transient pain inflicted by forceps wresting salvation out of an impending doom.

To keep that in mind is our, as Europeans, joint responsibility.

18

DOES THE RICHNESS OF THE FEW BENEFIT US ALL?

28 January 2013

A most recent study by the World Institute for Development Economics Research at the United Nations University reports that the richest one percent of adult humans alone owned 40 percent of global assets in the year 2000, and that the richest 10 percent of adults accounted for 85 percent of total world wealth. The bottom half of the world's adult population owned one percent of global wealth. This is, though, but a snapshot of the on-going process. Yet more and more bad and ever worse news for equality of humans, and so also for the quality of life of all of us, is lining up daily.

'Social inequalities would have made the inventors of the modern project blush of shame' – so Michel Rocard, Dominique Bourg and Floran Augagner conclude in the article 'Human species, endangered' they co-authored and published in *Le Monde* of 3rd April 2011. In the era of the Enlightenment, during the lifetimes of Francis Bacon,

Descartes or even Hegel, in no place on earth was the standard of living more than twice as high as in its poorest region. Today, the richest country, Qatar, boasts an income per head 428 times higher than the poorest, Zimbabwe. And these are, let's never forget, comparisons between *averages* – and so akin to the facetious recipe for the hare-and-horsemeat paté: take one hare and one horse...

The stubborn persistence of poverty on a planet in the throes of economic growth fundamentalism is enough to make thoughtful people pause and reflect on the direct as much as the collateral casualties of that redistribution of wealth. The deepening abyss separating the poor and prospectless from the well-off, sanguine, self-confident and boisterous – an abyss of the depth already exceeding the ability of any but the most muscular and the least scrupulous hikers to climb – is an obvious reason to be gravely concerned. As the authors of the quoted article warn, the prime victim of deepening inequality will be democracy – as increasingly scarce, rare and inaccessible paraphernalia of survival and acceptable life become the object of a cutthroat rivalry (and perhaps wars) between the provided-for and the left-unaided needy.

One of the basic moral justifications for free market economics, namely that the pursuit of individual profit also provides the best mechanism for the pursuit of the common good, has been thereby cast in doubt and all but belied. In the two decades preceding the start of the latest financial crisis, across the great bulk of OECD nations, the real household incomes for the top ten percent grew much faster than for the poorest ten percent. In some countries, real incomes of those at the bottom have actually fallen. Income disparities have therefore widened markedly. 'In the US, the average income of the top ten percent is now 14 times the bottom 10 per cent' – feels obliged to admit Jeremy Warner, assistant editor of *The Daily Telegraph*, one of the dailies with a long record of enthusiastic affirmation of the dexterity and proficiency of the 'invisible hand' of markets trusted by editors and subscribers alike to resolve as many (if not more) problems as markets create. And he adds:

> Growing income inequality, though obviously undesirable from a social perspective, doesn't necessarily matter if everyone is getting richer together. But when most of the rewards of economic progress are going to a comparatively small number of already high income earners, which is what's been happening in practice, there's plainly going to be a problem.

That admission, gingerly and half-hearted as it sounds and feeling but no more than half-true as it in fact is, arrives on the crest of a rising tide of research findings and official statistics documenting the fast growing distance that separates those at the top from those at the bottom of the social hierarchy. In jarring opposition to political pronouncements intended to be recycled into a popular belief – no longer reflected upon, questioned and checked – the wealth amassed at the top of society has blatantly failed to 'trickle down' and make the rest of us any richer or feel more secure and more optimistic about our and our children's future, or happier.

The grand canyon

In human history, inequality with its all-too-visible propensity for extended and accelerated self-reproduction is hardly news. And yet what has recently brought the perennial issue of inequality as well as its causes and consequences back into the focus of public attention, making it into a topic of passionate debates and eye-opening departures?

The most seminal among the departures is the discovery, or rather the somewhat delayed realisation, that the 'big divide' in American, British, and a growing number of other societies 'is now less between the top, the middle and the bottom, than between a tiny group at the very top and nearly everyone else'. For instance, 'the number of billionaires in the US multiplied forty times in the 25 years to 2007 – whereas the aggregate wealth of the 400 richest Americans rose from $169 to $1500 billion'. After 2007, during the years of credit collapse followed by economic depression and rising unemployment, the tendency has acquired a truly exponential pace: rather than hitting everyone in equal measure as it had been widely expected and portrayed, the scourge proved to be ruggedly and tenaciously selective in the distribution of its blows: the number of billionaires in the US reached in 2011 its historical record to date of 1210, while their combined wealth has grown from $3,500 billion in 2007 to $4,500 billion in 2010.

'In 1990, you needed a fortune of £50 million to make it into the list of the 200 richest residents in Britain compiled annually by the *Sunday Times*. By 2008, that figure had soared to £430 million, a near-nine fold increase'. All in all, 'the combined wealth of the world's richest 1000 people is almost twice as much as the poorest 2.5 billion'. According to the Helsinki based World Institute for Development Economics, people in the richest one percent of the world population are now almost 2000 times richer than the bottom 50 percent. Having recently collated available estimates of global inequality, Danilo Zolo concluded that very little data is needed to dramatically confirm that the sun is setting on the 'Age of Rights' in the globalisation era. The International Labour Organization estimates that 3 billion people are now living below the poverty line, set at US$2 per day. John Galbraith, in the preface to the Human Development Report of the United Nations in 1998, documented that 20 percent of the world's population cornered 86 percent of all goods and services produced worldwide, while the poorest 20 percent of them consumed only 1.3 percent; whereas today, after nearly 15 years, these figures have gone from bad to worse: the richest 20 percent of the population consume 90 percent of the goods produced, while the poorest 20 percent consume one percent. It is also estimated that 40 percent of the world's wealth is owned by one percent of the world population, while the 20 richest people in the world have resources equal to those of the billion poorest.

No New Virginia

Ten years ago Glenn Firebough noted that a longstanding trend in world-wide inequality showed signs of reversing – from rising inequality across nations and a constant or declining inequality between nations, to declining inequality *across nations* and rising inequality *within them*. While the 'developing' or 'emergent' national economies scored a massive influx of capital-in-search-of new quick-profit promising 'virgin lands', populated by cheap and meek labour as yet uncontaminated by the bacillus of consumerism and ready to work bare-survival wages – workplaces in the 'developed' economies vanished at an accelerated pace leaving the local labour force in a fast deteriorating bargaining position. Ten years later François Bourguignon found out that, while planetary inequality (between national economies), if measured by the average income per head, continues thus far to shrink, the distance between richest and poorest national economies continues to grow, and internal income differentials inside countries continue to expand.

When interviewed by Monique Atlan and Roger-Pol Droit, the economist and Prix-Goncourt-laureate novelist Erik Orsenna summed up the message all such and many other similar figures convey. He insisted that recent transformations benefit only an infinitely small minority of the world's population; their genuine scale would elude us were we to confine our analysis, as we used to do still a decade ago, to the average gains of the top ten percent. To comprehend the mechanism of the presently on-going *mutation* (as distinct from a mere 'phase in a cycle'), one needs to focus on the top one percent, perhaps even 0.1 percent. Failing to do so, one would miss the true impact of the change, which consists in the degradation of 'middle classes' to the ranks of the 'precariat'.

That suggestion is confirmed by every study whether focusing on the researcher's own country or arriving from far and wide. In addition, however, all studies agree on yet another point: almost everywhere in the world inequality is growing fast and that means that the rich, and particularly the very rich, get richer, whereas the poor, and particularly the very poor, get poorer – most certainly in relative, but in a growing number of cases also in absolute terms. Moreover: people who are rich are getting richer just *because* they are rich. People who are poor get poorer just *because* they are poor. Nowadays, inequality goes on deepening by its own logic and momentum. It needs no more help or kick from outside – no outside stimuli, pressures, nor blows. Social inequality seems nowadays ever closer to turning into the first perpetuum mobile in history – which humans, after innumerable failed attempts, have finally managed to invent and set in motion. This is the second among the departures that obliges us to think about social inequality from a new perspective.

As long ago as in 1979, a Carnegie study vividly demonstrated what an enormous amount of evidence available at that time suggested and common life experience continued daily to confirm: that each child's future was largely determined by the child's social circumstances, by the geographical place of its birth and its parents' place in the society of its birth – and not by its own brains, talents, efforts, dedication. The son of a big company lawyer had then a 27 times greater chance than the son of an on-and-off employed minor official (both sons sitting on the same bench in the same class, doing equally well, studying with the same dedication and boasting the same IQ) that by the age of forty he would be paid a salary putting him in the top ten percent of the richest people in the country; his classmate will only have a one in eight chance of earning even a median income. Less than three decades later, in 2007, things got much worse – the gap has widened and deepened, becoming less bridgeable than ever before. A study by the Congressional Office Bureau has found the wealth of the richest one percent of Americans to total $16.8 trillion, two trillion more than the combined wealth of the bottom 90 percent of the population. According to The Center for American Progress, during those three decades the average income of the bottom 50 percent of Americans grew by 6 percent – while income of the top one percent increased by 229 percent.

In 1960, the average pay after taxes for chief executives at the largest U.S. corporations was 12 times greater than the average wage of factory workers. By 1974, the CEO's salaries and perks had risen to about 35 times that of the company's average worker. In 1980 the average CEO was already making 42 times as much as the average blue-collar worker, doubling ten years later to 84 times. But then, about 1980, a hyper-acceleration of inequality took off. By the mid-1990s, according to *Business Week*, the factor was already 135 times as big; in 1999 it had reached the 400-fold level and in 2000 jumped again to 531. And these are but a few of fast growing numbers of similar 'facts of the matter' and figures attempting to grasp them, quantify and measure. One can go on infinitely quoting them, as there is no shortage of new figures which each and every successive research adds to the mass already accumulated.

Two worlds in one

What are, however, the social realities which those figures reflect?

This is how Joseph Stiglitz sums up the revelations brought up by the dramatic aftermath of the two or three arguably most prosperous decades-in-a-row in the history of capitalism that preceded the 2007 credit collapse, and of the depression that followed: inequality has always been justified on the grounds that those at the top contributed more to the economy, performing the role of 'job creators' – but 'then came 2008 and 2009, and you saw these guys who brought the economy to the brink of ruin walking off with hundreds of millions of dollars'. Most obviously, you couldn't this time justify the rewards in terms of their beneficiaries' contribution to society; what the latter contributed was not new jobs, but the lengthening lines of '*redundant people*' (as the jobless are now dubbed – not without sound reasons). In his latest book *The Price of Inequality*, Stiglitz concludes that the US has become a country 'in which the rich live in gated communities, send their children to expensive schools and have access to first-rate medical care. Meanwhile, the rest live in a world marked by insecurity, at best mediocre education and in effect rationed health care'. This is a *picture of two worlds* – with few if any interfaces or meeting points between them, and so also with their inter-communication all but broken (in the US as much as in Britain, families have started to set aside an ever greater part of their income to cover the costs of living geographically as well as socially away, the further away the better, from 'other people', and particularly the poor among them).

In his sharp and brilliant vivisection of the present state of inequality, Danny Dorling, the Sheffield University Professor of Human Geography, puts flesh around the bones of Stiglitz' skeleton synthesis – while raising simultaneously the perspective from a one-country to the planetary level: the poorest tenth of the world's population regularly go hungry. The richest tenth cannot remember a time of hunger in their family's history. The poorest tenth can only rarely secure the most basic education for their children; the richest tenth are concerned to pay sufficient school fees to ensure that their children need only mix with their so-called 'equals' and 'betters' and because they have come to fear their children mixing with other children. The poorest tenth almost always live in places where there is no social security, no unemployment benefit. The richest tenth cannot imagine themselves ever having to try to live on those benefits. The poorest tenth can only secure day work in town, or are peasants in rural areas; the richest tenth cannot imagine not having a secure monthly salary. Above them, the top fraction of a percent, the very richest cannot imagine surviving on a salary rather than on the income coming from the interest that their wealth generates.

And he concludes: 'as people polarise geographically, they begin to know less and less of each other and imagine more and more'... While in his most recent statement titled 'Inequality: the real cause of our economic woes', Stewart Lansley falls in with Stiglitz's and Dorling's verdicts that the power-assisted dogma meriting the rich with rendering society service by getting richer is nothing more than a blend of a purposeful lie with a contrived moral blindness: according to economic orthodoxy, a stiff dose of inequality brings more efficient and faster growing economies. This is because higher rewards and lower taxes at the top – it is claimed – boost entrepreneurialism and deliver a larger economic pie.

Inequality lies hurt us all

So has the 30-year experiment in boosting inequality worked? The evidence suggests no. The wealth gap has soared, but without the promised economic progress. Since 1980, UK growth and productivity rates have been a third lower and unemployment five times higher than in the more egalitarian post-war era. The three post-1980 recessions have been deeper and longer than those of the 1950s and 1960s, culminating in the crisis of the last four years. The main outcome of the post-1980 experiment has been an economy that is more polarised and more prone to crisis.

Having noted that 'falling wage shares suck demand out of economies which are heavily dependent on consumer spending' and in effect 'consumer societies lose the capacity to consume', and that 'concentrating the proceeds of growth in the hands of a small global financial elite leads to asset bubbles', Lansley comes to an inevitable conclusion: harsh realities of social inequality are bad for everyone or almost everyone within society. And he suggests a sentence that ought, yet thus far did not, to have followed such a verdict:

> the central lesson of the last 30 years is that an economic model that allows the richest members of society to accumulate a larger and larger share of the cake will eventually self-destruct. It is a lesson, it appears, that has yet to be learned.

To learn that lesson we need and to learn it we must – lest we reach a point of no return: a moment when the current 'economic model', having emitted all the warnings of approaching catastrophe while failing to capture our attention and to prompt us to act, fulfils its 'self-destructive' potential. Richard Wilkinson and Kate Pickett, themselves the authors of an eye-opening study *The Spirit Level: Why More Equal Societies Almost Always Do Better*, point out in their jointly written 'Foreword' to Dorling's book, that the belief in 'paying the rich huge salaries and bonuses' being right because of their 'rare talents' 'benefitting the rest of society' is a straightforward lie. A lie which we can swallow with equanimity only at our own peril – and, eventually, at the cost of our own self-destruction.

Since the appearance of Wilkinson's and Pickett's study the evidence of the detrimental, quite often devastating impact of high and rising levels of inequality on pathologies in human cohabitation and the gravity of social problems has all but accrued and goes on accruing. The correlation between high levels of income inequality and a growing volume of social pathologies has by now been amply confirmed. A growing number of researchers and analysts point out, however, that in addition to its negative impact on the quality of life inequality has also an adverse, halting effect on economic performance; instead of enhancing it, it holds it down. In the already quoted study, Bourguignon picks some of the causes of the latter phenomenon – as depriving the potential entrepreneurs of access to bank credits because of their lack of collateral the creditors require, or rising costs of education that strip the talented youngsters of the chances to acquire the skills needed to develop and apply their abilities. He adds the negative impact of the rise in social tension and the ambiance of insecurity – the fast growing costs of security services eating into the resources that could be turned to better economic uses.

And so, to sum up: is it not true what so many of us believe, and what all of us are pressed and nudged to believe while all-too-often feeling tempted, and inclined, to accept? Is it true that 'richness of the few benefits us all'? It is not true, in particular, that all and any tampering with the natural inequality of humans is harmful to the health and vigour, as well as to the creative and productive powers of the society which each and every human member of society has vested interests in magnifying and holding at the highest conceivable level. And it is not true that the differentiation of social positions, capacities, entitlements and rewards reflects the differences in natural endowments and in the contributions of its members to the well-being of society. A lie is the most loyal of allies (or is it a foundation?) of social inequality.

19

THE CHANGING NATURE OF WORK AND AGENCY

9 January 2014

There are, no doubt, many – perhaps uncountable – unresolved issues that will demand close watching during the coming year and press us for bold decisions and fateful steps. They are too numerous and most of them are too grave for my attempt to provide their full inventory to be anything but to say the least presumptuous and to smack of irresponsibility. I confine myself therefore to only two, though as I believe deserving quite an honourable place among our preoccupations.

Jerzy Kociatkiewicz, my colleague teaching at the University of Sheffield, shared with me a few days ago the following observation:

Last year, various beef and pork products sold in UK supermarkets were found to contain horsemeat. The continuing investigation was remarkable not because of uncovered dishonesty and profiteering (we have come to expect these in any story of corporate misconduct), but because it laid bare just how little managerial oversight there is in the global economy of subcontractors.

By coincidence, a couple of days ago BBC4 broadcast a 'Hidden Killers' documentary, revealing among other things half-forgotten worries of the past, like exploding toilets or spontaneously combusting clothes, that between 1831 and 1854 (that is, before health and safety legislation was imposed and a workable control system was started in earnest) had been found in Britain in 2,500 products 'from aluminum compounds in bread to lead chromate in mustard'.

Almost two centuries later, the plague of food adulteration allegedly put paid to once and for all by efficacious management and ostensibly long buried worries, is rising from beneath the (mock, apparently) gravestones. The question is, how did it happen? Not a marginal question, judging by the massiveness of its resurrection; also in view of the 'managed society' having qualities of a hologram or a stem cell: every part reflects the totality and from each one every other fragment can be extrapolated and restored.

Changing nature of managerial strategies and work

During most of the modern era, managerial strategies as recorded and articulated in Max Weber's ideal type of bureaucracy were focused on rendering behaviour of their subordinates utterly predetermined and therefore predictable through eliminating or suppressing all and any factors of influence other than the commands issued by the superiors; those strategies involved as their major tenet the repression or at any rate suspension by the subordinates of their personal idiosyncrasies (beliefs, predilections, affectations, mannerisms and eccentricities – as well as loyalties, commitments and obligations) for the duration of performing the tasks set by their superiors – collated with the reduction of the criteria by which their performance was measured and judged down to the single yardstick of 'the job having been done as commanded'.

The side effect of such strategies – not necessarily deliberately chosen and time and again experienced as uncomfortably and vexingly cumbersome – used to be the assumption by the managers of an undivided responsibility for the consequences of the command on the objects of commanded action. Released thereby from their responsibility *for* the results, their subordinates were in exchange burdened with the undivided responsibility *to* their superiors issuing the command.

The liquid phase of modernity brought in its wake a *sui generis* 'return of the depressed'. In the preceding 'solid' or 'hard' phase the managers used to record individual idiosyncrasies of the managed on the side of *liabilities*. With a huge investment of mental and physical energy, money expenditure and sheer ingenuity, managers tried (with but a mixed success, to be sure) to repress those liabilities and better still to extirpate them altogether, as factors throwing out of balance routine and uniformity, the two pillars of an instrumentally-rational performance and so also of a smooth and unswerving goal-pursuit.

The same individual idiosyncrasies, resenting routine and resisting uniformity, singularities and peculiarities of the managed, are now transferred onto the *assets* pages of accountancy books. Rather than to be suffered and reluctantly endured as no less inescapable than undesirable facts of life taxing and sapping the potential profitability of the enterprise, they are now welcome as ushering into as yet unexplored expanses of opportunity and so an augury and possibly a warrant of unprecedented gains. The side effect of that new managerial strategy is the shifting of responsibility *for the results* onto the shoulders of the managed, simultaneously reducing the responsibilities of the managers to the selection of the managed according to the promise of profitability they hold for the enterprise – and to the evaluation of quality (measured first and foremost in financial terms) of what they deliver.

Knowing of such seminal departures in the practical meaning of management and in the distribution of responsibilities, one shouldn't be astonished, let alone surprised, when learning 'how little managerial oversight there is in the global economy of subcontractors'.

Presenteeism

That seminal shift in the practice of management could not be accomplished nor would have been conceivably designed were it not for the thorough deregulation of the labour market and conditions of employment and a retreat from the practice of collective bargaining and collectively negotiated salaries, wages and terms of employment: in other words, the thorough and well-nigh comprehensive *individualisation* of the employer-employee relations. At least three of the side effects of that underlying shift have been hugely consequential for the ensuing managers' position, role and strategy.

First, the management of situational uncertainty is now to a fast growing extent turning into a task of the managed instead of the managers.

Second, the managed have been cast in a setting that favours mutual competition and rivalry instead of solidarity.

Third, being increasingly reduced to hire-and-fire acts and progressively stripped off continuous top-down surveillance and supervision, the bonds between the managers and the managed have been substantially weakened: a departure that allows to disguise a massive growth of exploitation (instead of purchasing specific skills and specified time of the managed, managers now can – and try hard to, with considerable effect – claim use of the totality of time and all the explicit or hidden, known or yet to be found and/or elicited abilities and potentials of their employees) as 'growing autonomy' of the managed and 'flexibility' of their working times.

The suspicion of a massively contrived *trompe d'oeil* has, however, found a recent confirmation in the research report of Professor Cary Cooper of Lancaster University. It follows from his study that

> around 40 percent of people are accessing emails on holiday – that's work ... (S)taff want to show that they are committed to try and keep their job in the next wave of redundancies.

Cooper coined the term 'presenteeism', as well as another term 'electronic face time' for its email variety, to denote that fast spreading tendency for the 'flexibility of office time' to generate huge volumes of free – unpaid and unrecorded – overtime. That tendency has already become enough of a public secret to be given – openly, explicitly, without beating about the bush – an official stamp by Marissa Mayer, the new boss of Yahoo, in a message addressed to her employees: working from home is 'not what's right for Yahoo right now ... Come into the office where we can see you, and look busy'...

So where are we now, at the threshold of 2014? On the eve of another U-turn in the history of modern management? A signal of retreat from a bridge too far, back to the old trusty because familiar ways and means of having things done through forcing other people to do them? Or, rather, what we seem to be facing is stripping the new managerial philosophy and practice of the no longer needed disguise – a disguise apparently successful enough to work itself by now out of its job? In disguise of emancipation and new freedoms we have been successfully re-drilled to be 24-7 at the beck and call of our employers and forget about the once gallantly defended boundary separating the private from the office time. The bluff of the scam can now be safely called.

Who Is Going To Do It?

Another participant in our threesome electronic conversation about the present and foreseeable future of management, Professor Monika Kostera of the University of Warsaw, raised an issue seemingly different yet in fact closely related to the one above: we presently are, she suggested, in a phase of 'interregnum',

> a phase in-between systems, in between working organisational and institutional orders, able to offer political, economic and cultural frames for human culture to function and develop, and also to cultivate a sustainable relationship with the broader ecosystem. It is a liminal period, of unknown durability, characterised by fundamental uncertainty and many compelling questions, in place of what up till now has been regarded as axiomatic truth, ceteris paribus of modern economic faith.

New working ideas of power and political settings, of markets – financial and human, and of planetary consequences of ecological and social mismanagement are being urgently called for and the areas of problems caused by the lack of viable solutions are growing to ever more alarming proportions. The current system is perfectly unable if perhaps not completely unwilling to solve them.

Interregnum – the condition in which the old ways and means of getting things done have stopped already working properly yet the new, more effective ways and means are still at the designing stage or at best in the stage of experimentation – has its temporal, to wit 'diachronic', but also its spatial, that is 'synchronic' dimension. Calling our present condition an 'interregnum' we refer to a time-span of yet unknown length, stretching between a social setting which has run its course and another, as yet under-defined and most certainly under-determined, which we expect or suspect to replace it.

But we also refer to processes under way in the morphology of human togetherness, the structure of human cohabitation: old structures, so to speak, are falling apart, its fragments enter new and untested arrangements, emergent settings are spattered with blank spots and ill-fitting fragments in an advanced stage of disrepair, as well as with other zombie-like fragments, still mobile though out of joint and lacking obvious uses and applications: the condition typical of 'failing systems'.

Incapacitated by the logic of 'more of the same', extant systems are, as Monika Kostera rightly concludes, 'perfectly unable' to face up to the challenge of de- and particularly re-composition. The structures that once interlocked into something reminiscent of a 'system' are now, clearly, in disarray. But structures' function is to serve as catapults as well as guiding/steering frames for action. In the state of disarray they are, indeed, 'perfectly unable if perhaps not completely unwilling' to assure that such a function is performed. Hence the big, perhaps the biggest question of the time of interregnum, fully and truly the 'meta-question' – one that needs to be answered in order for all the rest of the questions to be properly articulated and the search for answers to them started: 'Supposing that we know what needs to be done, who is going (i.e. able and willing at the same time) – to do it?'

Seeking an optimally convincing answer, Kostera focuses on what she names the 'meso level' of social integration. She wonders

> how we can make a difference on the meso level by practices of self-management and self-organisation, not waiting for the politicians or corporations for initiative but by taking the initiative into our own hands. In the world of complete colonisation of almost all human domains by management, in a world where virtually everyone has been educated in management in some form, at some point in our lives; we have all learned the basics of how to manage. I propose that it is time to use that knowledge to create meso structures – organisations – able to support themselves economically, that have other overarching aims than the current mainstream corporations and political institutions.

Choosing to pinpoint an agency capable of meeting the required standard halfway between the state and the realm of individually run life politics, Kostera is on the right track.

She is right in disqualifying the uppermost level – the level of territorially sovereign nation states – and the lowest level, that of the individual- or family-centred life politics, as serious, dedicated and reliable candidates for the job. I fully agree with her verdict.

The sovereignty illusion

Territorial sovereignty – the relic of the 1648 Westphalian settlement signed in Münster and Osnabrück yet for the duration of the nation-building and imperial colonialism eras presumed to remain the universal precept on the world order and practiced as such – has by now, in the era of global interdependency, turned into an illusion. As to the postulated/assumed sovereignty of the individual, it had been an illusion from its birth – a figment of imagination of governments keen to shoulder off the protective obligations of the state. Though for different reasons, the actors operating at levels above and below the medium level of social integration are equally unfit for the job.

The 'medium level' stretching betwixt and between those extremes is of course a fairly vast territory, densely populated and encompassing a variegated multitude of formations. Not all of them are promising enough to deserve investing in them hopes for the resurrection of effective agency. At the moment, I am inclined to follow, however, the trail blazed by Benjamin Barber in his as provocative as it sounds convincing study/manifesto published last year by Yale University Press under the title *If Mayors Ruled the World: Dysfunctional Nations, Rising Cities*.

Today, states Barber,

after a long history of regional success, the nation state is failing us on the global scale. It was the perfect political recipe for the liberty and independence of autonomous peoples and nations. It is utterly unsuited to interdependence. The city, always the human habitat of first resort, has in today's globalising world once again become democracy's best hope.

Why nation states are singularly unfit to tackle the challenges arising from the fact of our planet-wide interdependence? Because 'too inclined by their nature to rivalry and mutual exclusion', they appear 'quintessentially indisposed to cooperation and incapable of establishing global common goods'. Why the cities, especially the big cities, are immensely more adapted to take the lead? Because of

the unique urban potential for cooperation and egalitarianism unhindered by those obdurate forces of sovereignty and nationality, of ideology and inequality, that have historically hobbled and isolated nation-states inside fortresses celebrated as being 'independent' and 'autonomous'. Nor need the mayors tie their aspirations to cooperation to the siren song of a putative United Nations that will never be united because it is composed of rival nations whose essence lies in their sovereignty and independence.

In fact, as Barber emphatically points out, far from being a utopian fantasy, all this is already happening – unplanned, unsupervised, unmonitored; it happens spontaneously, as a natural phase in the development of cities as locations where 'creativity is unleashed, community solidified, and citizenship realised'. Daily confronted by globally generated problems and the urge to resolve them, cities are already proving their ability to address 'multiplying problems of an interdependent world' incomparably quicker and better than the offices of nation state capitals. To cut a long story short:

> Cities have little choice: to survive and flourish they must remain hospitable to pragmatism and problem solving, to cooperation and networking, to creativity and innovation.

More than any other 'totalities' on the present-day planet, cities are capable of meeting that challenge point blank. Whether they like it or not, cities and particularly the largest among them serve as dustbins in which the globally produced problems are disposed and where they ultimately land. And whether they like it or not, they function as laboratories in which effective tools to tackle and methods to resolve those problems are daily designed and put to test.

City states

Cities are also of the right size and density of habitation to efface or at least seriously mitigate the difference between imagined and experienced totalities, between administration and human interaction, and eventually between physical and moral density. Peaceful, mutually beneficial and gratifying coexistence between different traditions, cultural choices or creeds is happening when subject to the logic of urban life less a utopia and more a matter of daily work and achievement than in any other social setting. Cities indeed seem the best bet to all of us wishing for an agency able and willing to rise to the challenges of a globalised, multicultural and multi-centred planet.

Well, another societal challenge of enormous consequence. Facing up to the full grandiosity of a challenge, let alone finding an adequate response, is likely to take much longer than one year. Finding out whether the response was indeed adequate would take immensely more time yet. But here we are, *homini sapienti*, squeezed between an increasingly irrelevant past and stubbornly recondite future and known for being wise after the fact more often than before.

20

THE CHARLIE HEBDO ATTACK AND
WHAT IT REVEALS

13 January 2015

You went through the tragedies of the 20th century – two wars, Shoah, Stalinism. What's the specific nature of the Islamic extremist threat we're facing today, in your view?

Political assassination is as old as humanity and the chances that it will be dead before humanity dies are dim. Violence is an un-detachable companion of inter-human antagonisms and conflicts – and those in turn are part and parcel of the human condition. In various times, however, political murders tended to be aimed at different kinds of victims.

A hundred years or so ago it was targeted mostly against politicians – personalities like Jean Jaures, Aristide Briand, Abraham Lincoln, Archduke Ferdinand and countless others; ideologically varied, located at different points of the political spectrum yet all belonging to the category of current or future power holders. It was widely believed at that time that with their death the world (or the country) will turn away from what was viewed as the cause of grievance, and toward something better – a more friendly and comfortable condition.

On 11th September 2001 political assassinations were directed not against specific, identifiable and named political 'personalities' in the political limelight, or for that matter against people held personally responsible for the wrongdoings the assassins pretended to punish, but against institutions symbolising economic (in the case of the World Trade Centre) and military (in the case of the Pentagon) power. Notably, a centre of spiritual power was still missing in the combined political operation.

There were two aspects of the Charlie Hebdo murders that set them apart from the two previous cases:

First: on 7th January 2015 political assassins fixed a highly media-visible specimen of mass media. Knowingly or not, by design or by default, the murderers endorsed – whether explicitly or obliquely – the widespread and fast gathering public sense of effective power moving away from political rulers and towards the centres viewed as responsible for public mind-setting and opinion-making. It was the people engaged in such activities that the assault was meant to point out as culprits to be punished for causing the assassins' bitterness, rancour and urge of vengeance.

And second: alongside shifting the target to another institutional realm, that of public opinion, the armed assault against *Charlie Hebdo* was also an act of personalised vendetta (going back to the pattern set by Ayatollah Khomeini in his 1989 Fatwa imposed on Salman Rushdie). If the 11th September atrocity chimed in with the then tendency to 'depersonalise' political violence (following the *pour ainsi dire* 'democratisation' of violence by mass-media publicity that divided its attention according to the quantity of its – mostly anonymous and incidental – victims, and the volume of spilt blood), the 7th January barbarity crowns the lengthy process of deregulation – indeed the 'de-institutionalisation', individualisation and privatisation of the human condition, as well as the perception of public affairs shifting away from the management of established aggregated bodies to the sphere of individual 'life politics'. And away from social to individual responsibility.

In our media-dominated information society people employed in constructing and distributing information moved or have been moved to the centre of the scene on which the drama of human coexistence is staged and seen to be played.

A lot has been said about this attack: a prosecution of the holy wars between Christians and Muslims, an assault on freedom of expression, a symbolic challenge to Paris as the cradle of Western values. What do you think?

Each of the causes suggested to have their part in inflaming the Christian – Muslim antagonism contains a grain of truth but none offers the whole truth. Many factors contribute to this profoundly complex phenomenon. One of them, perhaps the most decisive, is the ongoing diasporisation of the world, which results in transforming the distant stranger, or briefly visiting stranger, or passing-by stranger, into a next-door neighbour – sharing the street, public facilities, workplace and school. The close proximity of the stranger always tends to be somewhat unnerving. One doesn't know what to expect from a stranger, what his or her intentions are, how would s/he respond to one's gambit. More important yet, one cannot – unlike when moving around the securely 'online only' world – skip over the all-too-real differences, often jarring and repellent, manifesting at close quarters their incompatibility with one's habitual, and thus feeling homely, cozy and secure, mode of being.

How do we react to that situation? The snag is that we've failed thus far to develop, let alone to entrench, a satisfactory response. The strategy widely seen as progressive is a policy known under the name of 'multiculturalism'. In his *Trouble with Principle* Stanley Fish distinguished two varieties of that strategy: a 'boutique' and a 'strong' multiculturalism. Boutique multiculturalism, as Fish defines it, is a superficial fascination with the Other: ethnic food, weekend festivals, and high-profile flirtations with the Other. Boutique multiculturalism is exactly what all this global consumerism nonsense in the Facebook status message means. Purveyors of this superficial brand of multiculturalism appreciate, enjoy, sympathise with, and 'recognise the legitimacy' of cultures other than their own. But they always stop short of approving these radically. 'A boutique multiculturalist', Fish suggests, 'does not and cannot take seriously the core values of the culture he tolerates'. By the same token, I'd say, s/he adds offence to the injury: a humiliation to the wound, the offence of disregarding or flatly rejecting what the 'stranger' next door holds sacrosanct; humiliation of a jovial and benevolent dismissal of a 'you can't be serious, you can't mean it' kind. Fish wrote:

> The trouble with stipulating tolerance as your first principle (...) is that you cannot possibly be faithful to it because sooner or later the culture whose core values you

are tolerating will reveal itself to be intolerant at that same core. The distinctiveness that marks it as unique and self-defining will resist the appeal of moderation or incorporation into a larger scale. Confronted with a demand that it surrender its viewpoint or enlarge it to include the practices of its natural enemies – other religions, other races, other genders, other classes – a beleaguered culture will fight back with everything from discriminatory legislation to violence.

It is in the nature of offence and humiliation to seek an outlet, through which it can be discharged, and a target. And when it so happens, as it does all around an increasingly diasporised Europe, that the boundaries between humiliating and the humiliated overlap with the boundaries between socially privileged and socially deprived, it would be naïve not to expect that both the outlets and the targets are avidly sought and keenly pinpointed. We presently live on a minefield of which we know (or at least we should) that it is spattered with explosives. Explosions occur, though there is no way to predict when and where.

Radical Islamic ideology or economic 'structural' inequalities: what component plays a major role in determining this phenomenon of radicalisation and terrorism in Europe and the world?

Why do you reduce the issue of 'radicalisation and terrorism in Europe' to the phenomenon of 'radical islamic ideology'? In *Soumission*, Michel Houllebecq's second grand dystopia sketching an alternative (to the triumph of individualised consumers) path to disaster, the 2022 French elections are won by Mohammed Ben Abbes following a neck-and-neck race with Marine Le Pen. The tandem is anything but accidental. Prophetic? It could happen like this, in case we are unable or unwilling to change course.

Hopes for freedom of self-assertion and for arresting the rise of social inequality, invested in democracy, blatantly failed to realise. Democratic politics and, yet more, the trust in democracy as the best road to the solution of the most haunting social problems are in crisis. As Pierre Rosanvallon argues,

> Those in power no longer enjoy the confidence of the voters; they merely reap the benefits of distrust of their opponents and predecessors.

All around Europe we witness a rising tide of anti-democratic sentiment – and a massive 'secession of plebeians' (in their current reincarnation as precarians) to the camps located on the opposite extremes of the political spectrum though promising in unison to replace the already discredited high-mindedness with yet to be tried high-handedness of autocracy. Spectacular acts of violence may be seen as reconnaissance sallies into that. The word of the Prophet, the spokesman of Allah, is just one of the banners deployed to rally the humiliated and deprived, left behind and abandoned, cast-out and excluded, frightened, angry and vengeance-seething desperadoes.

You asserted ethics always needs an 'I', not a 'We'. That's the opposite of fundamentalism. Is the 'I', the affirmation

of individual identity, the way for ethics to defeat fundamentalism?

In his first *Esortazione Apostolica*, Pope Francis restored the lost-from view moral dimension to our submission – surrender – to the licentious, unbridled, left of social leash capitalism, dazzled by its lust for gain and blind to human misery. You won't find a more profound and comprehensive answer to your question:

> In our time humanity is experiencing a turning-point in its history, as we can see from the advances being made in so many fields. We can only praise the steps being taken to improve people's welfare in areas such as health care, education and communications. At the same time we have to remember that the majority of our contemporaries are barely living from day to day, with dire consequences. A number of diseases are spreading. The hearts of many people are gripped by fear and desperation, even in the so-called rich countries. The joy of living frequently fades, lack of respect for others and violence are on the rise, and inequality is increasingly evident. It is a struggle to live and, often, to live with precious little dignity. (...)
>
> Just as the commandment 'Thou shalt not kill' sets a clear limit in order to safeguard the value of human life, today we also have to say 'thou shalt not kill' to an economy of exclusion and inequality. Such an economy kills. How can it be that it is not a news item when an elderly homeless person dies of exposure, but it is news when the stock market loses two points? This is a case of exclusion. Can we continue to stand by when food is thrown away while people are starving? This is a case of

inequality. Today everything comes under the laws of competition and the survival of the fittest, where the powerful feed upon the powerless. As a consequence, masses of people find themselves excluded and marginalized: without work, without possibilities, without any means of escape. (...)

Human beings are themselves considered consumer goods to be used and then discarded. We have created a 'throw away' culture which is now spreading. It is no longer simply about exploitation and oppression, but something new. Exclusion ultimately has to do with what it means to be a part of the society in which we live; those excluded are no longer society's underside or its fringes or its disenfranchised – they are no longer even a part of it. The excluded are not the 'exploited' but the outcast, the 'leftovers'.

Nothing to add, nothing to detract.

Fragments of this interview were first published in Italian in Corriere della Sera.

21

FLOATING INSECURITY SEARCHING FOR AN ANCHOR

6 January 2016

The Shorter Oxford English Dictionary defines 'security' as 'condition of being protected from or not exposed to danger'; but, at the same time, as 'something which makes safe; a protection, guard, defence': this means, as one of those not common (yet not uncommon either) terms that presume/hint/suggest/imply, an organic and so once and for all sealed unity of the condition with the assumed means to attain it (a sort of unity akin to that which for instance is suggested by the term 'nobility').

As the *condition* to which this particular term refers is highly and deeply as well as unquestionably appreciated and yearned for by most language users, the approbation and regard bestowed on it by the public rubs off thereby on its acknowledged *guards* or *providers*, also called 'security'. Means bask in the glory of the condition and share in its indisputable desirability. This having been done, a fully predictable pattern of conduct follows, just as in the habit of all conditioned reflexes. Do you feel insecure? Press for more public security services to guard you and/or buy more security gadgets believed to avert dangers. Or: people who elected you to high offices complain of feeling insufficiently secure? Hire/appoint more security guards, allowing them also more liberty to act as they consider necessary – however the actions they might choose are unappetising or downright loathsome and revolting.

Social securitisation

A heretofore unknown in socio-political discourse, and still unrecorded in its dictionaries available in bookshops, term 'securitisation' has appeared quite recently in debates. What this imported term is meant to grasp and denote is the ever more frequent reclassification of something as an instance of 'insecurity', followed well-nigh automatically by transferring that something to the domain, charge and supervision of security organs. Not being of course the cause of such automatism, the above mentioned semantic ambiguity makes it no doubt easier.

Conditional reflexes can do without lengthy argument and laborious persuasion: the authority of Heidegger's '*das Man*' or Sartre's '*l'On*' ('this is how things are done, aren't they?') renders them so obvious and self-evident as practically unnoticeable and unavailable for questioning. Conditioned reflex stays itself, safely, unreflected upon – in safe distance from the searchlights of logic. This is why politicians gladly resort to the term's ambiguity: making their task easier and their actions assured *a priori* of popular approval even if not of promised effects, it helps the politicians to convince their constituencies of taking their grievances seriously and acting promptly on the mandate those grievances have been presumed to bestow.

Just one example – picked up off-cuff from the most recent headline news. As *Huffington Post* reported shortly after the night of terrorist outrages in Paris,

> French President Francois Hollande said a state of emergency would be declared across France and national borders shut following a spate of attacks in Paris on Friday evening (...) 'It is horrifying', Hollande said in a brief statement on television, adding that a cabinet meeting had been called.
>
> 'A state of emergency will be declared,' he said. 'The second measure will be the closure of national borders,' he added. 'We must ensure that no one comes in to commit any act whatsoever, and at the same time make sure that those who have committed these crimes should be arrested if they try to leave the country,' he added.

The *Financial Times* reported the same presidential reaction under a no-beating-about-the-bush title: 'Hollande's Post-Paris Power Grab':

> President François Hollande declared the national emergency immediately after the Nov. 13 attacks. It allows police to break down doors and search houses without a warrant, break up assemblies and meetings, and impose curfews. The order also clears the way for military troops to be deployed to French streets.

The sight of broken down doors, of swarms of uniformed police officers breaking up meetings and entering homes without asking their residents' agreement, of soldiers patrolling the street in the broad daylight – they all make a powerful impression as demonstrations of the government's resolution to go the whole hog, down to 'the heart of the trouble' and to allay or altogether disperse the pains of insecurity haunting their subjects.

Latent and manifest functions

Such demonstration of intentions and resolve is, to use Robert Merton's memorable conceptual distinction, its 'manifest' function. Its 'latent' function, however, is quite opposite: to promote and smooth up the process of 'securitising' the plethora of people's economic and social headaches and worries born of the ambiance of insecurity generated by the frailty and fissiparousness of their existential condition. The above-mentioned sights are after all guaranteed to create the atmosphere of a state of emergency, of the enemy at the gate – of the country and so also my own home facing mortal danger; and bound as well to firmly entrench those 'up there' in the role of the providential shield barring the danger from falling on both.

Whether those sights' manifest function has been successfully performed is, to say the least, a moot question. Acquitting itself brilliantly from their latent function is not, however, left to doubt. The effects of the Head of State flexing his (and of the security organs he commands) muscle in public were as fast coming as they were exceeding all previous attainments by the current holder of the presidential office, heretofore found by opinion polls as the least popular president in France since 1945. A fortnight or so later Natalie Ilsley could sum those effects up under the saying-it-all title 'After Paris, Hollande's Popularity Soars to Highest Level in Three Years':

One poll revealed on Tuesday an 'unprecedented' 20-point rise in the president's confidence rating to 35 percent in December—a level not seen since December 2012. According to French daily newspaper Le Figaro, results by polling agency TNS Sofres show that 35 percent of French people say they trust Hollande to deal with the aftermath of the attacks claimed by the Islamic State militant group (ISIS), an increase from 13 percent polled in August (...) Another poll published on Tuesday by Ifop-Fiducial for French weekly Paris Match and Sue Radio also showed a dramatic increase in support for Hollande. Based on the views of 983 French citizens, Hollande's approval rating soared from 28 percent in November to 50 percent in December.

The widespread sense of existential insecurity is a hard fact: a genuine bane of our society priding itself, through the lips of its political leaders, on the progressive deregulation of labour markets and 'flexibilisation' of work and, in the end result, notorious for the growing fragility of social positions and instability of the socially recognised identities, as well as for unstoppably expanding the ranks of the precariat (a novel category, defined by Guy Standing primarily as quicksands on which they are forced to move). Contrary to many an opinion, such insecurity is not just a product of politicians pursuing electoral gains or media profiting of the panic-mongering broadcasts; it is true, however, that the real, all-too-real insecurity built into the existential condition of ever expanding sections of population is welcome grist to the politicians' mill. It is in the process of being converted into a major – perhaps even paramount – stuff of which present-day governing is fashioned.

Governments promote anxiety

Governments are not interested in allaying their citizens' anxieties. They are interested instead in beefing up the anxiety arising from the future's uncertainty and constant and ubiquitous sense of insecurity – providing that the roots of that insecurity can be anchored in places which provide ample photo opportunities for ministers flexing their muscles while hiding from sight the rulers overwhelmed by the task with which they are too weak to cope. 'Securitisation' is a conjurer's trick, calculated to do just that; it consists in shifting anxiety from problems which the governments are incapable of handling (or are not keen to try), to problems which the governments may be seen, daily and on thousands of screens, to be eagerly and (sometimes) successfully tackling.

Among the first kind of problems there are such principal factors of the human condition as the availability of quality jobs, reliability and stability of social standing, effective protection against social degradation and immunity against a denial of dignity – all such determinants of the safety and well-being which the governments, once promising full employment and comprehensive social security, are nowadays incapable of pledging, let alone delivering. Among the second, the fight against terrorists conspiring against the ordinary folks' bodily safety and their cherished possessions easily grasps and holds fast the first fiddle: all the more so because of its chance of feeding and sustaining the legitimation of power and the votes-collecting effort for a long time to come; after all, the ultimate victory in that fight remains a distant (and thoroughly doubtful) prospect.

Viktor Orban's laconic and tremendously catching

dictum 'all terrorists are migrants' provides the sought-after key to the government's effective struggle for survival – all the more so thanks to the implicitly smuggled suggestion of the symmetry of the link – and so the overlap between the two linked categories. Such an interpretation defies logic – but faith does not need logic to convert and hold minds; on the contrary, it gains in holding power as it loses in its logical credentials. For the ears of governments wishing to redeem, against all odds, their seriously lopsided and sinking *raison d'être*, it must sound as a horn of a salvage-boat sailing out from the dense, impenetrable fog in which the horizon of their survival struggle has been wrapped.

Orban et orbi

For the author of that dictum, the gains were immediate, while outlays all but limited to a 4 metre-high fence along a 177 km border with Serbia. When the Hungarian respondents were asked in the December Medián-HVG poll what comes into their minds when they hear the word 'fear', more people (23 percent) named terrorism than illness, crime, or poverty. Their overall sense of security has fallen considerably. 'The respondents also had to indicate their feelings on a number of statements and mark the intensity of these feelings on a scale of 0-100. For example, 'immigrants pose health risks for the native population' (77), 'immigrants substantially increase the danger of terrorist attacks' (77), 'those who illegally cross the borders will have to serve a jail sentence' (69). The statement that 'immigration might have a beneficial effect on Hungary because it would remedy the demographic problems and would add to the labour force' elicited little enthusiasm (24). Expectedly, Orban's fence proved enormously popular. While in

September 68 percent of the population approved it, now 87 percent of the population stand behind Viktor Orban's solution to the migrant problem – and so by proxy, let's make it clear, to the haunting spectre of insecurity.

We may risk guessing that, if coupled with a focus on a specific, visible and tangible adversary, an intensification of fear is somehow more endurable than are dispersed, floating fears of unknown origin. It may even prove to be, perversely, a satisfactory experience: once we decide that we are up to the task, we willy-nilly acquire vested interest in its grandiosity: the more it appears awesome and indomitable, the more proud and flattered we tend to feel. The more powerful and scheming the enemy, the higher the heroic statuses of those who declare war on him. No coincidence that an absolute majority of Hungarian respondents approved of the statement: 'Certain unnamed outside moving forces are behind the mass migration'.

Calling the nation to arms against an appointed (as Carl Schmitt suggested) enemy gives an added advantage to the politicians in search of voters: it is bound to rouse the nation's self-esteem and earn thereby the nation's gratitude – at least of the (growing, or afraid to grow) part of the nation pained by a damaged, eroded or altogether withdrawn recognition and self-respect, and therefore yearning for some (even if inferior because cumulative and so depersonalised) recompense for the loss of personal dignity.

Finally, the policy of 'securitisation' helps to stifle our, the bystanders', pangs of conscience at the sight of its victims; it 'adiaphorises' the migrants issue (exempts them, that is, from moral evaluation), putting those victims, once they have been cast in public opinion in the category of would-be terrorists, outside the realm of moral responsibility – and above all outside the realm of compassion and the impulse to care. Many people feel – knowingly or not – relieved of responsibility for the fate of the wretched as well as of the moral duty that otherwise would inevitably follow to torment the bystanders. And also for that relief – knowingly or not – many people are grateful.

Victims' false guilt

As Christopher Catrambone wrote a few days ago in *The Guardian*,

> Following the terror attacks in Paris and political scaremongering that followed, we have started putting these people at risk again. The human tragedy of people fleeing by sea to escape terrorism is being diminished by vitriolic accusations, the building of walls, and a fear that these refugees are coming to kill us. Most are just escaping war in the Middle East. But even when trapped between European anger and the violence that drove them out of their country, refugees still brave the worsening seas.

Catrambone is not a panic-monger, he knows the fate of people on the receiving side of 'securitisation' better than most of us, being a member of MOAS (the Migrant Offshore Aid Station). According to the statistics compiled by that charitable search-and-rescue organisation, 'the drowning of men, women and children fleeing war, poverty and oppression at sea remains a daily occurrence: since August 2014 MOAS has rescued almost 12,000 people from the water'. Catrambone alerts and appeals:

> The EU is predicting that 3 million refugees and migrants will have reached its territory by 2017. This will have a

positive impact that will stimulate the economy. Ultimately that is why people are coming, will continue to come and cannot be stopped from coming to Europe. They seek the same thing we all want: something better. The reality is that these people will contribute to, not take away from, our economy. Yes, it will be rough in the beginning, but they are becoming part of Europe's future, whether we like it or not.

One more comment is in order. On top of being morally callous and odious, socially blind as well as to a large extent groundless and intentionally misleading, 'securitisation' can be charged with playing into the hands of the recruiters of genuine (as distinct from falsely accused) terrorists. 'A new study by the intelligence consultancy Soufan Group puts the figure at approximately 5,000 fighters from EU origins' thus far recruited by Daesh', as Pierre Baussand of the Social Platform puts it (only two attackers in Paris have been identified as non-European residents). Who are those young people fleeing Europe to join the terrorist cohorts and planning to return after receiving terrorist training?

Baussand's well-argued answer is that 'the majority of Western converts to Daesh come from disadvantaged backgrounds'. A recent Pew Research Center study found that,

> European millennials have suffered disproportionately from their countries' recent economic troubles [...] In the face of this challenge, young Europeans often view themselves as victims of fate.

Such widespread disenfranchisement across society goes some way to explaining the allure of the sense of importance and control that Daesh instils in its supporters.

'Rather than caving in to reactionary, misinformed populist rhetoric such as that of far-right organisations, equating all migrants with terrorists', Baussand warns, 'our leaders must (...) reject 'us versus them' stances and the surge in Islamophobia. This only plays into the hands of Daesh, who use such narratives as recruitment tools'.

Reminding us this way that 'social exclusion is a major contributor to the radicalisation of young Muslims in the EU', and having repeated after Jean-Claude Juncker that 'those who organised these attacks and those that perpetrated them are exactly those that the refugees are fleeing and not the opposite', Baussand concludes:

> While there is no doubt about the role the Muslim community must play in eradicating radicalisation, only society as a whole can tackle this common threat to us all (...) Rather than waging war on Daesh in Syria and Iraq, the biggest weapons that the West can wield against terrorism are social investment, social inclusion and integration on our own turf.

This is, I suggest, a conclusion demanding our close 24/7 attention, and urgent – as well as resolute – action.

22

NO MORE WALLS IN EUROPE: TEAR THEM DOWN!

27 July 2016

Professor Bauman, it seems like new walls are rising again in Europe. The reasons politicians push for the decision to build these walls – either real or 'bureaucratic' – refer to the issues of migration and security. How do you judge what is happening? What are the risks in this rush to 'securitisation' of the continent?

We need to study, memorise, and do our best do draw practical conclusions from Pope Francis's analysis (in his 'thank you' speech on the occasion of receiving the European Charlemagne prize) of the mortal dangers signalled by 'new walls rising in Europe'; walls raised – paradoxically and disingenuously – with the intention/hope of cutting out small plots of land safe for its residents from the hurly-burly world full of risks, traps and menaces. Having pointed out that 'creativity, genius and a capacity for rebirth and renewal are part of the soul of Europe', that in the last century Europe bore witness that 'a new beginning was indeed possible' – and in the effect 'laid the foundation for a bastion of peace, an edifice made up of states united not by force but by free commitment to the common good and a definitive end to confrontation' so that 'Europe, so long divided, finally found its true self and began to build its house' – Pope Francis notes, with deep concern and sorrow, that if 'the founding fathers of united Europe' – 'heralds of peace and prophets of the future' – inspired us 'to build bridges and tear down walls', the family of nations they prompted to create seems of late

> to feel less at home within the walls of the common home. At times, those walls have been built in a way varying from the insightful plans left by the original builders. Their new and exciting desire to create unity seems to be fading; we, the heirs of their dream, are tempted to yield to our own selfish interests and to consider putting up fences here and there.

People seem to be more and more scared by the series of attacks that are happening in our cities. Whatever the real reasons behind these attacks – which may vary – the perception is one of a growing level of insecurity. How can politics address this fear without falling in a witch-hunting scheme?

The roots of insecurity you mention go deep; they are sunk in our mode of existing, marked by weakening inter-human bonds, the crumbling and falling apart of communities, the tendency to recast our common social problems into individually suffered worries – and 'subsidiarising' the task of fighting them to the bereaved individuals left to stew in their own juices. Our uncertainty and the resulting sense of insecurity are existential: they are born and daily reborn out of the ongoing replacement of human solidarity with mutual suspicion and cutthroat competition. The fear they beget is diffuse and spread over all aspects of our life pursuits and therefore unanchored, seeking vainly a target on which it could be focused – a palpable, visible target within reach, one that we could try to control. But in our (selectively) globalised world, a playground of powers emancipated from political control and powerless politics incapable of controlling them, the gap between the grandiosity of tasks and mediocrity of tools to handle them and perform with them is widening; the 'natural habitat' of existential insecurity, the space subjected to the vagaries of deregulated, let off-the-leash and politically uncontrolled economic powers, continues thereby to widen too – and so does the thirst for a reduction of the unbearable complexity of any challenge to a simple, possibly instant, shortcut measure and for strong leaders who as irresponsibly and deceitfully as boisterously and bombastically promise to apply in exchange for unconditional obedience of their subjects.

The EU seems to be divided in its response to the migration problem. It also seems to be divided on issues like security – Viktor Orban has asked the EU to follow Trump's model in this. Is the dream at the very root of the European Union about to be destroyed by these forces?

All in all, we are witnessing today throughout Europe a

worrisome tendency to reclassify urgent socio-political issues as the problems of the security organs and policing. It does not spell well for the spirit that inspired the founding and the expansion of the European Union. After all, a major, perhaps the defining feature of that spirit was the vision of Europe in which military and policing security measures will gradually but steadily and consistently become redundant.

From Trump to the EU, fear seems to dominate the political discourse. Is our society destined to be dominated by fear?

This is indeed a sombre and upsetting prospect (though by no means a predetermined, inescapable destiny). Promises of demagogues are catching, but fortunately short-lived. Once new walls have been built, more armed guards deployed on airports and in public places, more refugees refused asylum and more migrants deported, their irrelevance to the genuine roots of our uncertainty and the fears and anxieties they generate will become, fortunately, transparent. Deregulated market forces will go on playing havoc with all and any of our existential certainties. Demons that haunt us (fear of losing our place in society, suspected fragility of our life-achievements, the menace of social degradation and exclusion) won't evaporate and disappear. We may come back to our senses and acquire immunity to the siren songs of the haranguers and rabble-rousers striving to build political capital on leading us astray. The big question, however, is how many people will need to fall victim and find their lives wasted before this happens.

Religion – particularly Islam – is more and more indicated as a factor that can stop integration. In Germany, movements like Pegida openly describe Islam as the mask of throat-cutters. How do you think societies and politicians might operate to prove this equation wrong?

Let's avoid the dangerous mistake of extrapolating long-term tendencies (let alone inevitable futures) from current fads and foibles. As the uniquely perspicacious German sociologist Ulrich Beck suggested, at the bottom of our present confusion lies the discrepancy between finding ourselves already cast in a 'cosmopolitan situation' (being doomed to cohabit permanently with different cultures, ways of life, faiths) – and the lagging far behind in the urgent task of the development and appropriation of 'cosmopolitan awareness'. Putting paid to that discrepancy – bridging the gap between the realities in which we live and our capacity to understand their logic and requirements – is not a task to be performed overnight.

To sum up our current predicament, let me again quote from the impeccable insights of Pope Francis. In the already referred-to speech, he confessed:

> I dream of a Europe where being a migrant is not a crime, but a summons to a greater commitment on behalf of the dignity of every human being ... I dream of a Europe that promotes and protects the rights of everyone, without neglecting its duties toward all. I dream of a Europe of which it will not be said that its commitment to human rights was its last utopia.

And he asked:

What has happened to you, the Europe of humanism, the champion of human rights, democracy and freedom? What has happened to you, Europe ... the home of poets, philosophers, artists, musicians, and men and women of letters? What has happened to you ... the mother of great men and women who upheld, and even sacrificed their lives for, the dignity of their brothers and sisters?

These questions are addressed to all of us; to us, who – as humans are and can't but be in all times and all places – are made by history while making it, knowingly or not. It is up to us to find answers and give them; in deeds as much as in words.

I believe that the most awesome obstacle to finding the answers is our dilatoriness in seeking them.

This interview was conducted by Davide Casati and first published in abbreviated form in Corriere della Sera (in Italian).

23

TRUMP: A QUICK FIX FOR EXISTENTIAL ANXIETY

14 November 2016

Amongst the 'liberal left', in the UK and USA, there's a major response to Donald Trump's electoral success: fear. 'This is a moment of great peril', 'Donald Trump's victory challenges the western democratic model'; he will 'carry us into a different political era, a post-neoliberal, post-end-of-history politics, than any other imaginable president...'; 'the election of Donald Trump to the Presidency is nothing less than a tragedy for the American republic, a tragedy for the Constitution...'. Do you agree with this sort of apocalyptic response?

Apocalyptic visions crop up whenever people enter the Great Unknown: being certain that nothing, or not much will continue as it heretofore was, while having little if any inkling of what is bound to or likely to replace it.

Reactions to Trump's victory, as you know, were instant

and prolific but, amazingly, they were all but consensual: very much like in the case of the Brexit vote, ascribing the Trump vote to a popular protest against the political establishment and political elite of the country as a whole, with which a large part of the population had grown frustrated for failing to deliver on its promises. No wonder that such interpretations were most common among the liberals, who hold the strongest vested interests in the maintenance of the present political establishment.

Not being part of that elite, never having occupied any elected office, coming 'from outside the political establishment' and at loggerheads even with the party of which he was formally a member (rejoining in 2009 after a five-year stay with the Democrats), Trump represented a splendid and unique occasion for such a wholesale condemnation of an entire political system – just as in the British referendum, where all major political parties (Conservatives, Labour and Liberals) united in their call to remain in the EU and so one could use his/her single vote to record his/her distaste for the political system in its entirety.

Another (or rather complementary) factor all too often cropping up in the instant commentaries was the notable hunger of the population for the replacement of the endless but ineffective and impotent parliamentary bickering with the indomitable and unassailable will of a 'strong man' (or woman) and his/her determination and capability to impose right away, without prevarication and procrastination, the quick fixes, shortcuts and instant solutions of his or her choice. Trump skilfully construed his own public image as a person of such qualities of which large parts of the electorate dreamt.

These were surely not the only factors contributing to Trump's triumph – but surely crucial and perhaps the principal ones. Clinton's thirty-year long membership of the establishment and her half-way, wishy-washy, piecemeal agenda militated, on the contrary, against her as the right and popular choice.

What I believe we are currently witnessing is a thorough re-hashing of allegedly untouchable principles of 'democracy' (though I don't think that the term itself will be abandoned) as the name of the political ideal; that *signifiant*, as Ferdinand de Saussure would have branded it, has been absorbing and is still capable of parenting many and different *signifiés*. There is, for instance, a distinct possibility of the traditional safeguards (such as Montesquieu's division of power into three autonomous – legislative, executive and judiciary – sectors, or the British 'checks and balances' system) falling out of public favour and being stripped of significance, replaced explicitly or matter-of-factly by condensation of power within an authoritarian or even dictatorial model. The cases you've named are some of the multiplying symptoms of a tendency to – so to speak – bring power from the nebulous elitist heights where it has been placed or has drifted 'closer to home': into a direct communication between the strong (wo)man at the top and the aggregate of their supporters/subjects, equipped with 'social websites' as media for indoctrination/opinion surveys.

Although Trump focused on racial/nationalist issues, his appeal was not entirely based on ethnic nationalism. Many analysts have already emphasised that, apart from a set of regressive attitudes towards difference, the most valuable calling card for Trump has been the economic anxiety of US citizens who have been feeling marginalised by globalisation. The two aspects – economic

anxiety and anxiety towards the Other – are linked together. How?

The trick was to connect the two: make one of the two, inseparably intertwined and beefing up each other. And this was precisely what Trump, a trickster supreme (though by no means alone on the world's political stage) has managed to achieve. I am inclined even to step further beyond the oft-mentioned marriage of identity politics and economic anxiety – to suggest that Trump managed to condense all aspects/sectors of existential uncertainty that haunt whatever has remained of the old working class and former 'middle' classes, and indoctrinate the sufferers that removal of strangers, ethnic aliens, asylum-seekers and other foreign newcomers was the dreamt-of 'quick fix' which would put paid to *all* anxiety in one fell swoop.

Some of the people who voted for Trump belong to the category of the 'expelled': those who were part of a 'social contract' and have been marginalised or pushed out of it, and those who have never been and have no hope to be part of it in future (what Bonaventura de Sousa Santos referred to as 'post- and pre-contractualism'). Do you agree with those academics, like Saskia Sassen, who claim that Trump's victory represents the end of the inclusive model of the post-war Keynesian economic model, in favour of a model marked by an opposite trend, expulsion?

The passage from an inclusivist to exclusivist worldview, mindset and policy is everything but new. It has been closely synchronised with another qualitative leap – from a society of producers to a society of consumers, one which can't exist without marginalisation: setting apart an 'underclass' not just degraded in, but exiled from the society of classes, or a category of 'flawed consumers' unfit to be readmitted. The current trend of the 'securitisation' of social problems adds grit to the same mill: it casts the nets of exclusion yet wider while relegating its catch from the category of lesser, though still benign quality, to a more sinister, because toxic – morbid and murderous – division.

In some of your books, for example in *In Search for Politics*, you have analysed what you call the 'wicked trinity' - uncertainty, insecurity and vulnerability - the feelings of people living in a world where a divorce has occurred between power and politics. Does this divorce inevitably lead to the request for a 'strong man' and to populism?

Yes, I'm inclined to believe so. The divorce you mention leaves a gap – a frighteningly widening gap – from which the poisoning mixture of hopelessness and haplessness emanates. The orthodox and so familiar and believed-to-be-available instruments of effective fighting back the troubles and anxieties are no longer believed to be capable of delivering on their promises. To a society in which fewer and fewer people remember, first hand, the charms of living under a totalitarian or dictatorial regime of the yet-untried strong (wo)man this seems not a poison, but an antidote: because of their pretended, assumed or ascribed capability of getting things done, instant solutions, quick fixes and immediate effects they promise to carry in their dowry.

Beppe Grillo, the leader of the Italian *Movimento Cinque Stelle* (Five Stars Movement), wrote a brief comment after the victory of Trump, emphasising the similarities between his own party's success in Italy and the success of Trump in the USA, stating: 'Those who dare, the stubborn, the barbarians, will bring the world forward. And we are the barbarians!'. Now, we are used to judge all anti-establishment forces as forms of populism. Don't you think that too often populism is a *passe-partout* label, used by a self-confident establishment in order to avoid the task of having to understand who the barbarians are, and what they actually want? Should Trump's election be interpreted also as a message to the 'establishment'?

In Europe, Grillos are currently thick on the ground. To those whom civilisation has failed, barbarians are the saviours. Or this is what they lean over backwards to convince the gullible of being. Or this is what the abandoned and neglected in the distribution of the civilised gifts ardently desire to believe. Some establishments might be eager to grasp that opportunity, just as some believers in posthumous life are sometimes eager to commit suicide.

This is the edited version of an interview with Giuliano Battiston first published in l'Espresso.

24

HOW NEOLIBERALISM PREPARED THE WAY FOR TRUMP

16 November 2016

I still vividly remember what fewer and fewer people, as time goes by, can and do: the names that Nikita Khrushchev, having decided to expose and publicly decry and condemn the crimes of the Soviet regime to prevent their repetition, gave to the moral blindness and inhumanity which was until then its mark: he called them 'mistakes and deformations', committed by Joseph Stalin in the course of the successful implementation of essentially healthy, correct and deeply ethical policy.

In Khrushchev's many hours-long speeches no room was found for the slightest suspicion that there must have been some inequity, indecency and immoral malignance with which that policy was from the start adulterated and poisoned; and which – unless arrested and thoroughly revised – had to lead to the now denunciated and decried atrocities. The system's norm was presented and a series of blunders committed by one man, at best in cooperation with some others, also personally nameable.

I also remember vividly public reactions to Khrushchev's revelations. Some people, brought up, drilled and groomed as it were under the wardenship of the Soviet Ministry of Truth, embraced and accepted, even if not without some residual unease, the successive proclamations from on high. More people cried, bewailing the historical drama of their lives for the second time – but this time degraded to the rank of (contingent, and surely unintended) gaffes and oversights of an in essence unerring man of integrity pursuing an unqualifiedly noble goal. But most people laughed, though the bitterness in that laughter was all too audible.

I am not recalling all those (and after all, distant) events just because old people like me tend to be fond of, and addicted to, reminiscences – but also due to their eerie similarity to the reactions of the defeated and their sympathisers to the resounding drubbing administered to Hillary Clinton, the Democratic Party she represented, and the neoliberal policies they mistakenly conducted and promised to continue after their electoral victory. Even terms like 'mistakes' or 'deformation', with the names of the culprits duly attached, are assigned in both compared reactions the role of paramount – sufficient and satisfactory – explanation.

Orban, Kaczynski, Fico, Trump – this is an incomplete list of those who have already managed or are about to make it – that is, to impose a rule that has its sole (and sufficient!) foundation and legitimation in the will of the ruler; in other words, to put into practice Carl Schmitt's (once a pretender to the role of Adolf Hitler's court philosopher) definition of sovereign power (see his *Political Theology*) as a 'decisionist' rule. The list

of those who watch avidly their audacious and brazen inso-
lence, while full of admiration and itching to follow their
examples, is lengthening – and fast. Alas, the public acclaim
and demand for the first and for the second, and therefore for
the principle of *Ein Volk, ein Reich, ein Führer* put in words by
Hitler in 1935 and into flesh promptly thereafter, is growing as
fast – and perhaps yet faster. Until recently a supply market
for would-be 'one and only' leaders has turned quickly, and
thus far unstoppably, into a market of demand. Trump
became the President of the US because he made it clear to
Americans that he will be that kind of a leader *and* because
Americans wanted to be led by a leader of that kind.

Absolutism and liberalism

A 'decisionist' leader needs nothing except a (spontaneous
or contrived, voluntary or imposed) public acclaim to act.
His decisions bear no other constraints – not even the ones
supposedly derived from and/or imposed by genuine or
putative 'higher reasons' or supreme, indisputable super-
human commandments – as in the case of divinely anointed
monarchs of the Middle Ages. A decisionist leader comes
close to the absolute: as God in his reply to Job's questioning, he refuses to explain his decisions and reject Job's (or
anybody else for that matter) right to ask for explanation
and expect it to be given. The sole explanation the leader's
resolution required, and was owed to those affected and
given to them, is the leader's will.

The 'certainty' of things important to life happening or
not is the most avid of dreams dreamed by people harassed
and oppressed by their uncertainty (though that certainty
might also be, as William Pitt the Younger observed already
in 1783, 'the plea for every infringement of human freedom'

and 'the argument of tyrants'). Politics guided by the decisionist principle is the meeting point between the tasty arguments of tyrants and the ravenous appetite of their acclaimers. The new era of liberal democracy whose imminent advancement Pitt was one of the first to adumbrate was to be, we may say, dedicated to preventing such a meeting, for the sake of reason and genuine human interests, from happening.

In the course of the subsequent decades merging into centuries, law theorists and practitioners as well as philosophers of politics joined forces in order to achieve – and once achieved, safeguard – that purpose. To the pursuing of that objective was their thought and ingenuity deployed. Road to fulfilling the purpose (identified for all practical intention with the passage of power from the kings and princes to people) led in prevailing opinion through institutional measures: division between legislative, executive and judiciary sectors of power, simultaneously mutually autonomous and closely, intimately dovetailed – pressing them thereby to permanently engage in negotiation of agreement, while drawing away from the temptations of solitary, potentially absolute, rule.

That tendency was complemented by another – of more cultural than institutional provenance. Its manifestation was the slogan *Liberté, Egalité, Fraternité* promoted by *les philosophes* of Enlightenment and shortly later embroidered on the banners carried from one end of Europe to another by French revolutionary armies. Advocates of that slogan were aware that its three elements stood chance of becoming flesh only together. *Liberté* could yield *Fraternité* solely in company with *Egalité*; cut off that medium/mediating postulate from the triad – and *Liberté* will most likely lead to *inequality*, and in effect to *division and mutual enmity and strife*, instead of unity and solidarity. Only the triad *in its entirety* is capable to secure a peaceful and so thriving society, well-integrated and imbued with the spirit of mutual cooperation.

Whether explicitly or implicitly, such a stance came into close association with the 'classic' liberalism of the next two centuries, which agreed that humans can be really free only on condition of possessing the capability of making use of their freedom – and only when *both* qualities, freedom and brotherhood, are obtained the true *Fraternité* may follow. John Stuart Mill drew from his thoroughly liberal convictions socialist conclusions; while Lord Beveridge, the moving spirit and agitator of the universal welfare state in Britain (as well as the inspirer of the rest of European countries to follow that example), considered and presented the pattern he recommended as indispensable for the implementation of indubitably liberal ideals.

Equality in exile

But to cut the long story short: neoliberalism, now the hegemonic philosophy shared by almost the whole of the political spectrum (and most certainly the entire part classified by Trump and his ilk as the 'establishment' earmarked for annihilation by the popular wrath and rebellion) distanced itself from its predecessor and indeed set itself in stark opposition by doing precisely what the classic liberalism fought valiantly to prevent while leaning over backward to reverse in case it was already done: and that by exiling the precept of *Egalité* – for all practical intents and purposes, from the three-partite compact of the Enlightenment's principles and postulates – even if not always from its entitlement to lip service.

After thirty/forty years of undivided and not seriously challenged hegemony of neoliberal philosophy in a country of great expectations and yet, courtesy of its neoliberal rulers, also of their no lesser frustrations, the electoral victory of Trump became all but pre-determined. Given the circumstances, the mistakes and deformations eagerly searched or construed and so hotly debated by most of the opinion-makers were at utmost left the role of icing the fully baked (over-baked?) cake.

For the self-appointed carriers of great expectations and conquerors of great frustration, demagogues and haranguers of all brands, in short: personages proclaiming themselves and believed to be strong (wo)men whose strength is measured by their capability of *breaking* rather than observing the rules of games foisted and cherished by the 'establishment', their common enemy – those circumstances amount to a field day. We (I mean and refer here to people worried by their actions and yet more by their not-yet-fully revealed potential), are advised, however, to be sceptical about quick fixes and instant exits from trouble. All the more so for the options we confront under those circumstances having been drawn from the category of choices between a devil and a deep blue sea.

Shortly before his death, the great Umberto Eco drew in his brilliant essay *Making an Enemy* the following sad conclusion from his numerous studies of the matter:

> Having an enemy is important not only to define our identity but also to provide us with an obstacle against which to measure our system of values and, in seeking to overcome it, to demonstrate our own worth.

In other words: we need an enemy to know who

we *are* and who we *are not;* knowing this is indispensable for our self-approval and self-esteem. And he adds: 'So when there is no enemy, we have to invent one'. A codicil: 'Enemies are *different* from us and observe customs that are not our own. The epitome of difference is the foreigner'.

Enemies within

Well, the trouble with a foreigner is that all too often he is indeed *foreign* – not just in the sense of obeying alien habits, but also – and most importantly – in that of residing beyond the realm of our sovereignty and so also beyond our reach and control. It is not fully up to us to make of such people enemies and put our enmity in practice (unless, of course, they cross boundaries with the intention of settling in our midst). If sovereignty consists in the 'decisionist' capacity of acting solely on one's own will, then many a foreigner is unfit to perform the role of a proper enemy according to Eco. In many cases (or perhaps in all?) it is better to seek, find or invent an enemy closer to home and above all inside the gate. An enemy within sight and touch is for many reasons more proficient (and above all easier to control and manipulate) than the seldom seen or heard member of an imagined totality. Already in the Middle Ages the function of the enemy in case of Christian states was perfectly performed by heretics, Saracens and Jews – all residing inside the realms of dynasties and churches by which they had been appointed. Today, in the era that favours exclusion over inclusion while the first (but not the second) is fast becoming a routine measure to which well-nigh mechanically to resort, internal choices assume yet more attraction and facility.

The most popular choice among the actual or aspiring

strong (wo)men when it comes to casting the enemy's role (that is, as spelled out by Eco, to the processes of self-defining, integration and self-asserting) – indeed a fully and truly meta-choice, determining all other choices by association or derivation – is currently *establishment*: un-packable as a foggy and (felicitously for their choosers and would-be foot soldiers) under-defined collection of have-beens who outlived their time and are grossly overdue to be relegated to history and recorded there in its annals as an aggregate of selfish hypocrites and inept failures. In a simplified rendition: establishment stands for the repulsive, off-putting and unprepossessing past, and the strong (wo)men, ready to send it to the rubbish tip where it belongs, stand for the guides to a new beginning, after which (s)he who has been naught shall be all.

∼

This is the final piece Zygmunt Bauman wrote for Social Europe - just a week after Trump's triumph.

Social Europe Editon

London, UK

ISBN 978-1-9997151-0-6

Cover design by Dan Mogford